New Approaches in Teaching History

TEACHING HISTORY TODAY AND IN THE FUTURE

About the Series

This series for K-12 and collegiate history teachers, educators, curriculum specialists, and preservice teacher education candidates provides information on current and future trends in the teaching and learning of history.

Books in the series explore the vast array of ideas, methods and strategies that actively engage students in learning historical content and developing skills that will help them in their education and to become competent citizens.

The volumes are aimed at professionals working or planning to work in history education at all levels of education in schools and other venues related to the teaching of history.

About the Series Editor

The **Teaching History Today and in the Future** was conceived by and is edited by Mark Newman, PhD, Professor of Studies Education, National College of Education, National Louis University, Chicago, Illinois.

Mark Newman has published articles and books on topics related to history, geography, and visual literacy. He received the 2022 Education Award from the International Visual Literacy Association and was awarded the National College of Education Distinguished Teaching Award in 2016. He has pursued his interest in history education through grants from the National Endowment for the Humanities and the Library of Congress Teaching with Primary Sources Program.

Titles in the Series

Teaching History Today: Applying the Triad of Inquiry, Primary Sources, and Literacy by Mark Newman

New Approaches in Teaching History: Using Science Fiction to Introduce Students to New Vistas in Historical Thought by Frederic Krome

New Approaches in Teaching History

Using Science Fiction to Introduce Students to New Vistas in Historical Thought

Frederic Krome

ROWMAN & LITTLEFIELD
Lanham • Boulder • New York • London

Published by Rowman & Littlefield
An imprint of The Rowman & Littlefield Publishing Group, Inc.
4501 Forbes Boulevard, Suite 200, Lanham, Maryland 20706
www.rowman.com

86-90 Paul Street, London EC2A 4NE

Copyright © 2024 by Frederic Krome

All rights reserved. No part of this book may be reproduced in any form or by any electronic or mechanical means, including information storage and retrieval systems, without written permission from the publisher, except by a reviewer who may quote passages in a review.

British Library Cataloguing in Publication Information Available

Library of Congress Cataloging-in-Publication Data

Names: Krome, Frederic, author.
Title: New approaches in teaching history: using science fiction to introduce students to new vistas in historical thought / Frederic Krome. Other titles: Using science fiction to introduce students to new vistas in historical thought
Description: Lanham: Rowman & Littlefield, [2024] | Series: Teaching history today and in the future | Includes bibliographical references. | Summary: "This book provides readers with a justification for using science fiction films and texts as a primary source for teaching history"—Provided by publisher.
Identifiers: LCCN 2023045447 (print) | LCCN 2023045448 (ebook) | ISBN 9781475869514 (cloth) | ISBN 9781475869538 (ebook)
Subjects: LCSH: History—Study and teaching—Audio-visual aids. | Science fiction—Study and teaching. | Motion pictures in education.
Classification: LCC D16.255.A8 K76 2024 (print) | LCC D16.255.A8 (ebook) | DDC 907.1—dc23/eng/20231219
LC record available at https://lccn.loc.gov/2023045447
LC ebook record available at https://lccn.loc.gov/2023045448

Contents

Preface: Opening New Vistas for Students by Using Science Fiction as a Primary Source — vii

Acknowledgments — xi

Introduction: Using Science Fiction Stories and Film in the History Classroom — 1

Chapter 1: Nationalism, Racism, and Imperialism in the Science Fiction of Jules Verne — 9

Chapter 2: Invaders from the Red Planet to We're the Martians Now: *War of the Worlds* in a Variety of Incarnations — 19

Chapter 3: Things to Come: The Fall and Rise of Civilization in the Future War — 29

Chapter 4: Science Fiction and the Holocaust—*Primary Source Analysis of a Future War Tale* — 49

Chapter 5: Mutations and Monsters: Cold War Anxiety in the 1950s and '60s — 63

Chapter 6: From *Starship Troopers* to *The Forever War* — 77

Chapter 7: From *Dune* to *The Ministry for the Future*: Environmentalism in Science Fiction—*Primary Source Analysis: A Photo Essay on the Atomic Battlefield* — 89

Chapter 8: Confronting the Color Line: Afrofuturism, Science Fiction, and Dissent — 103

Conclusion: A Brief How-To Guide — 111

Bibliography	117
About the Author	129

Preface

Opening New Vistas for Students by Using Science Fiction as a Primary Source

Using science fiction to teach history might seem counterintuitive. After all, to most casual observers, the genre seems to be more about predicting the future than exploring the past. Yet as Samuel Delany once asserted, science fiction (SF) is "not about the future. SF is in dialogue with the present. It works by setting up a dialogue with the here-and-now, a dialogue as rich and intricate as the writer can make it."[1] Science fiction author Ken MacLeod makes the relationship even more explicit: "History is the trade secret of science fiction, and theories of history are its invisible engine."[2]

In *1984*, George Orwell argues, "Who controls the past controls the future: who controls the present controls the past."[3] Conversely, when science fiction writers create a future, they are often using it to critique the present. A prime example of this is Margaret Atwood's novel, *The Handmaid's Tale*; set at an indeterminate point in the future, Atwood criticizes both our contemporary failure to deal with environmental issues, as well as the rising tide of religious fundamentalism that threatens women's rights.[4] Thus, by crafting a "history of the future," she is trying to influence the present. Properly evaluated, therefore, a science fiction text or film can be a valuable primary source, for it reveals the anxieties, hopes, and aspirations of an era.

This book asserts that science fiction literature and film are an underappreciated and untapped source for teaching history. The lack of interest in using the genre in the history classroom is somewhat surprising, given the popularity of science fiction, both visual and literary, in modern popular culture.

I teach at an open-access college, and a high proportion of students in my classes are underprepared. Finding material that can excite a student's curiosity, therefore, can be a key toward greater student engagement. Especially among students who are taking history as a requirement rather than from interest, the discovery that they can read or watch science fiction as part of their classwork often comes as a pleasant surprise.

Beyond its popularity, however, using science fiction for class assignments has certain pedagogical advantages: it introduces students to new vistas in historical thought, helps them learn how literature and film can be applied as a primary source, and can encourage participation with enjoyable projects.

This book is useful for secondary-level social studies and history teachers and university-level instructors who teach history or foundation courses in the humanities. This book provides instructors with both a conceptual framework for using science fiction literature and film in the classroom and with specific topics and exercises that can be easily aligned with student learning outcomes.

All instructors, on both the secondary and collegiate levels, are strapped for time. This book can enable teachers, especially those just entering the profession, to craft lectures, activities, and assignments that fit into the learning outcomes of such courses as US history, European history, and world history. By providing specific examples of sources—historical, literary, and cinematic—instructors can develop lesson plans to fulfill learning outcomes while expanding students' understanding of historical sources.

My interest in science fiction dates to my junior high school days, when I was an underachieving student with a possible learning disability. One of my instructors suggested that, instead of taking yet another battery of diagnostic tests, I should go to the library and find something of interest to me. I chose to read Robert Heinlein's *Farmer in the Sky*.[5] From that moment, I was a voracious reader, and within a short time, I had moved from being two years behind in reading comprehension to two years ahead of my classmates. It seems I did not have a learning disability; I was disinterested and bored.

My pedagogical interest in the genre developed somewhat later. When I joined the faculty at the University of Cincinnati Clermont College, my departmental colleagues fostered a culture of innovation in teaching that let me expand my pedagogical experimentation. I first used two episodes of the *Twilight Zone* more than twenty years ago in a course on the Holocaust and historical memory. From that point, I expanded my use of science fiction sources into other courses. Although some students were confused about why I was having them read a science fiction story or having them watch a sci-fi film for a history class, some seemed to enjoy the experience.

The introduction provides a justification for using science fiction texts and film in the history classroom, along with several pedagogical suggestions. Each chapter deals with a specific theme or historical era. The chapters begin with suggestions for constructing a contextual lecture for the students and a listing of possible texts or films to use and conclude with a set of practice discussion questions and assignments, along with a suggested reading list. This material can be adapted to both the traditional classroom and online learning. In addition, the conclusion offers suggestions on how teachers can develop sources and topics of their own that fit into their specific history curriculum.

NOTES

1. Quoted in Gary K. Wolfe, *The Known and the Unknown: The Iconography of Science Fiction* (Kent, OH: Kent State University Press, 1979), 18.

2. Ken MacLeod, *The Star Fraction* (New York: Tor, 2001), 11.

3. George Orwell, *1984* (London: Secker & Warburg, 1949), 44.

4. Margaret Atwood, *The Handmaid's Tale* (Toronto: McClelland and Stewart, 1985).

5. Robert A. Heinlein, *Farmer in the Sky* (New York: Scribner, 1950).

Acknowledgments

When I first interviewed for a position at the University of Cincinnati Clermont College, I told the search committee that I liked to use science fiction texts and films as primary sources in my courses; the committee apparently did not have a problem with the concept, which told me I was joining a faculty that was open to innovative approaches in the classroom. In the years since that interview, I have benefited from extended conversations on pedagogical issues from a diverse group of colleagues across multiple disciplines. Some of these discussions have also led to presentations at scholarly conferences.

One of the challenges of working at a teaching college is a demanding class schedule. My thanks to Lisa Mahl-Grisez, former associate dean of academic affairs at Clemont, for approving a course release in the spring of 2023 that enabled me to complete this manuscript. Lori Vine, my department program director, has saved me from Concur Hell on multiple occasions. Lori has also provided the wherewithal to use research funds to obtain source material crucial to the completion of this project.

I am grateful to the Clermont College librarians, past and current—Kathy Epperson, Rosemary Young, Katie Foran-Mulcahy, Katie Carslon, and Kathy Ladell—who have helped with interlibrary loans and the acquisition of books for research and teaching. The Public Library of Cincinnati and Hamilton County is a treasure trove for the history teacher. In addition to classic science fiction novels, the periodical section retained paper copies of Hugo Gernsback's *Electrical Experimenter* magazine and provided the images used in chapter 4.

My thanks to Mark Newman, series editor at Roman & Littlefield, for his welcoming attitude toward my initial proposal and his feedback on the draft manuscript. My thanks also to Jasmine Holman and the editorial production staff at the press steering the manuscript into production.

As with most book projects, I have relied on the advice and support of colleagues to work through methodical issues. Greg Loving (philosophy) and

Phoebe Reeves (English) listened to my ideas and provided feedback over many years of eating lunch together in those precious moments of free time between classes. Cassie Fetters (English) and I have discussed the various genres of science fiction, and she has also provided feedback on draft student assignments. The occasions when the four of us have taken our act on the road and presented at various conferences are among the high points of my academic career.

My spouse, Claire, often avers that she should not appear in the acknowledgments of my work. She has, however, endured many hours of watching science fiction films despite her preference for the murder-mystery genre. In addition, she has tolerated (barely) the mess of my home office, as I seem to be perpetually in the drive to finish my various projects.

I owe a special debt to my UC colleague John Brolley. When I first discussed this book project with him, John encouraged me to prioritize it. He then volunteered to read every chapter and provided crucial and humorous feedback on very short notice. He did all this despite running multiple programs and chairing various committees at the University of Cincinnati's Arts and Sciences College. That he did all this cheerfully helped maintain my morale through what turned out to be a frenetic month at the end of the last academic year.

Last, I want to remember my old friend James Westheider. Jim and I were roommates in grad school and remained close after finishing our degrees. I considered myself beyond fortunate when I was able to join him on the faculty at UC Clermont in 2007. Whenever I had what I thought was a harebrained idea, Jim encouraged me to pursue it and made himself available to talk through the difficult moments. Jim's passing in September 2020 has left a void in my life, both personal and professional.

An early version of some of the ideas discussed in this book first appeared in "Using Science Fiction Stories and Film in the History Classroom," *AURCO Journal* 26 (Spring 2020): 91–102. My friends have made this a better finished project than if I had done it alone. Any flaws that remain are my responsibility.

Introduction

Using Science Fiction Stories and Film in the History Classroom

Science fiction literature and film are often an underappreciated source for teaching history. This lacuna is somewhat surprising given the ubiquitous presence of science fiction, both visual and literary, in modern popular culture. Indeed, a cursory examination of the highest-grossing films of all time reveals that science fiction films are disproportionally represented in the top twenty-five, and as such, it is a safe assumption that most of our students have at the very least watched science fiction films at some point before entering college.[1]

At the postsecondary level, especially for those of us teaching at an open-access college with a high proportion of underprepared students, finding material that can excite a student's curiosity can be a key toward greater student engagement. Most importantly, when dealing with students at any level who are taking history as a requirement rather than from interest, the discovery that they can read a science fiction story or watch a science fiction film as part of their classwork often comes as a pleasant surprise.

Beyond its popularity, however, using science fiction for class assignments has certain pedagogical advantages: it introduces students to new vistas in historical thought, helps them learn how literature and film can be applied as a primary source, and can encourage participation with enjoyable projects. This book demonstrates how science fiction literature and film can enrich the teaching of history while providing teachers and students with methodological tools for the use of general historical sources, and it can potentially develop skills for a variety of courses within a history curriculum.

PEDAGOGY: INSTRUCTOR AND STUDENTS

While a number of historians—such as Richard Stites, Nicholas Cull, and Peter J. Bowler—demonstrate how to use science fiction in research, searching for pedagogy in the field reveals that the discussion is still in its infancy.[2] It is likely that the absence of any pedagogical exchange among historians is due to the fact that the academic study of science fiction is only about forty years old, and even today, the subject is still largely segregated within English, American studies, and popular culture studies programs.[3]

While literary scholars have engaged in instructional debates on teaching science fiction, to date the historian has few discipline-specific role models to follow.[4] Among the exceptions is A. Bowdoin Van Riper's *Teaching History with Science Fiction Films*.[5] Van Riper, however, focuses exclusively on American films and does little with literary sources. In addition, much of Van Riper's material is structured toward the creation of courses in which the focus is on the films. For the teacher of a survey history course, film can often be a supplement, but few instructors to date use it as a primary source specifically integrated into a history module.

This book is therefore part of an effort to rectify this omission. It uses examples drawn from several case studies from both foundation history courses and more advanced classes. As I show, most examples are easily integrated into such classes as modern European history, world history, and US history.

Science fiction novels and films need to be treated in the same manner as any other primary source employed in the classroom. Literature, whether short stories or novels, reveal attitudes, and the instructor and students need to be keenly aware of the standard approach to a source, with a few modifications:

- Who created the source?
- When was it created?
- If it was a film, in which type of venue—movie theater, television—did it first appear?
- If it is a text, what are the author's biases and perspective.

If material can be found on contemporary reaction to a literary text or film, all the better.

Instructors are fortunate that the use of film as a historical source in general incorporates pedagogical literature that can be mined to good effect. For example, an instructor unfamiliar with cinematic sources and the varieties of film can consult Paul Smith's edited volume *The Historian and Film* to learn how to identify and use film in the classroom.[6] In Smith's typologies, film is divided into three major groupings: feature film, actuality film, and documentary film:

1. **Feature (or fictional) film** is the most common type that the instructor will use when applying science fiction sources in the classroom. These films range from longer epics—James Cameron's *Avatar* (length: 3 hours, 36 minutes), for example—to shorter televisions shows, such as half-hour episodes of the *Twilight Zone*.
2. **Actuality film**, sometimes called film of record, ranges from home movies to material shot on location. Because science fiction is just that, fiction, these types of film have a limited utility for this study.
3. **Documentary films** are often a combination of source material, including actuality film, such as location shots and interviews with individuals, and feature films. For example, James Cameron's *History of Science Fiction* (2018, six episodes) is a thematic history of the genre that incorporates interviews with authors (actuality footage) with scenes from feature films representative of the specific subthemes within the genre. Episodes of this series are particularly useful for the instructor seeking to learn context; they can also be of use for students to provide historical context.

As with cinematic sources, the instructor must be cognizant of the changing nature of the literary world that produced science fiction texts. There is no consensus on the origins of the science fiction genre. While literary historian Adam Roberts sees its roots in antiquity and I. F. Clarke believes its start was in the late eighteenth century, other scholars feel that science fiction begam in the nineteenth century with the appearance of such iconic works as Mary Shelley's *Frankenstein* (1818) and the Extraordinary Voyages series of Jules Verne in the second half of the century.[7]

Rather than get too deeply involved in the debate, this study begins with some of Jules Verne's work, as he represents some of the most important ideologies of the era—such as nationalism and imperialism—and as such, his works are a user-friendly place to start.

In addition to the emergence of the genre, the instructor must be cognizant of the different venues in which science fiction texts have appeared. For example, almost all of Verne's Extraordinary Voyages series were originally serialized by his publisher Jules Hetzel in his magazine *Magasin*, and only after completion were they printed in book form. Now highly prized by collectors, even in the late nineteenth century, they were too expensive for most consumers, and Verne's popularity rested upon the magazine format.[8]

When using Jules Verne texts, it is also important to consider the specific learning outcome you are seeking to fulfill. If the lesson plan involves how nineteenth- and early-twentieth-century American audiences encountered the ideas Verne promoted in some of his iconic works, such as *20,000 Leagues under the Sea*, then having students read an early translated version makes sense.

Yet as such Verne scholars as Arthur Evans have demonstrated, contemporary English translations of Verne's work not only cut significant portions of text, but they also changed the meaning of the text itself, making the American experience of Verne much different from the original.[9] One example, which is used in chapter 1, is Verne's novel *The Begum's Millions*. Originally published in 1879, the earliest English translations even modified the title (*The Begum's Fortune*), in addition to cutting a number of passages and even changing the meaning of some words.[10] If the goal of a lesson is to have students understand Verne's use of nationalist rhetoric, stereotyping, and how a French author exacted a literary revenge on Germany in the immediate aftermath of the Franco-Prussian War (1870–1871), then the instructor is fortunate that a recent, full, and accurate translation into English is now available.

In addition to understanding the types of sources, the instructor likely needs some background on the genre's meaning and relevance to the history of ideas. Indeed, it is useful to a class discussion by starting with the well-worn truism that science fiction is written for scientists to the same extent that ghost stories are written for ghosts. Alternately derided and admired as an icon of popular culture, science fiction is, according to Heather Masri, a genre that is simultaneously historic and modern. Although its origins and indeed its very definition are the subject of scholarly dispute, over the past generation, a consensus has emerged that science fiction can best be understood as a field that intensely engages the contemporary world and its issues.[11] Science fiction writers are certainly cognizant of this relationship between past, present, and future. Writer Samuel Delany once asserted, "SF is not about the future. SF is in dialogue with the present. It works by setting up a dialogue with the here-and-now, a dialogue as rich and intricate as the writer can make it."[12] Ken MacLeod makes the relationship even more explicit: "History is the trade secret of science fiction, and theories of history are its invisible engine."[13]

Science fiction stories that deal with the future are conditioned by each writer's understanding of the past. Simply put, every story about the future is to some degree a projection of some aspect of the past and a speculation or extrapolation of the consequences of recent political, social, or technological developments. Professional historians often acknowledge that our understanding of the past is shaped by contemporary events, so introducing students to the concept that a society's sense of its future is also shaped by both our understanding of the past and our concerns with the present will help them link the study of science fiction with the study of history. In other words, science fiction is a fascinating window into the anxieties of a particular *historical* age, as it serves as everything from wish-fulfillment fantasies to warnings about a perceived crisis. For example, in his insightful analysis of revolutionary and utopian ideology in early Bolshevik Russia, historian Richard Stites argued that the "world of fantasy, like the world of myth and legend, reveals and evokes deep layers, archaic dreams and longings that better describe feelings and anxieties than some conventional acts of political adherence."[14]

A history of science fiction by literary scholar Roger Luckhurst is useful for the professor working to craft a background lecture. Luckhurst developed a typology of the conditions that led to the emergence of science fiction as a recognizable force in literature, and his work is particularly useful for the instructor because he explicitly delineates why the material is valuable for the student of history and literature. Luckhurst postulates four major factors leading to the emergence of the genre:

1. The growth of literacy in the Anglophone world after 1880, especially among the working classes.
2. The development of new and cheaper media (e.g., Northcliffe's penny press in Great Britain and pulp magazines in America).
3. The development of scientific and technical education, which expanded knowledge among the working classes.
4. The transformation of the physical world via technological innovations, which were clearly visible to the general population (e.g., the appearance of the automobile on city streets).[15]

These four factors inspired new notions about the future among the wider population, changing the existing intellectual assumption that the future would be similar to the present and the present was pretty much the same as the past. In addition to the transformation of ideas about the future, the expansion of education and growth of inexpensive printing also helps explain how culture evolved from a limited range of readers (who had access to expensive books) to a wider audience. By the dawn of the twentieth century, therefore, science fiction was an integral part of popular culture. So, for example, the instructor of a section on modern European history could have the students read H. G. Wells's iconic *War of the Worlds* and ask them to consider how it is a late-Victorian critique of imperialism.[16] Luckhurst focused on Britain, so the material is well suited to a European history class. With limited modifications, however, his typologies can also be applied to US and world history courses.

Each chapter in this volume focuses on a different theme, texts, and films. It provides information on the specific material that can be used in class; suggestions on lectures to provide context for the specific texts; and possible discussion questions, test questions, and writing assignments.

While popular culture artifacts—music, art, and images—are commonly deployed by history instructors to illustrate contemporary issues, using science fiction initially seems counterintuitive. Once the genre is recognized not just as an example of prognostication but also as a reflection of contemporary issues, then its use as a pedagogical tool becomes more logical. One of our jobs as students of history is to go back to the primary sources in our research, writing, and our teaching. Using primary sources and the historical controversies around them is a common theme in learning outcomes. There is, however, rarely (if ever) anything in our learning outcomes that prohibits us from employing material that students can regard as entertaining.

A NOTE ABOUT TOPICS AND SOURCES IN THIS VOLUME

At the risk of seeming defensive, it is important to mention what this volume does not do. It does not claim to be comprehensive in the history of science fiction, though to understand the source material, an engagement with much of the history of the genre is necessary. It also does not claim to be comprehensive in its coverage of texts and films discussed in the various chapters. In most cases the stories, whether in book form or published in serials, used in this volume are easily accessible, either because they remain in print or are accessible in digital formats. A similar rule about accessibility applies to the chosen films and television shows.

NOTES

1. Adam Roberts, "First Men and Original Sins," *Image*, no. 101 (Summer 2019), https://imagejournal.org/article/first-men-and-original-sins/. Roberts also lists which science fiction films are among the top money makers of all time.

2. See, for example, Peter J. Bowler, *A History of the Future: Prophets of Progress from H. G. Wells to Isaac Asimov* (New York: Cambridge University Press, 2017); Nicholas Cull, "Reading, Viewing, and Tuning in to the Cold War," in *The Cambridge History of the Cold War*, vol. 2, *Crises and Détente*, edited by Melvyn P. Leffler and O. A. Westad, 438–59 (New York: Cambridge: Cambridge University Press, 2010);

and Richad Stites, *Revolutionary Dreams: Utopian Vision and Experimental Life in the Russian Revolution* (New York: Oxford University Press, 1989), chap. 8.

3. See Andy Sawyer and Peter Wright, eds., *Teaching Science Fiction* (New York: Palgrave Macmillan, 2011) for examples.

4. For an example of curricula and syllabi that discuss using science fiction in English and American studies departments, see Miranda Corcoran, "Teaching History and Theory through Popular Culture: My First Time Designing a Module," US Studies Online, November 17, 2014, https://usso.uk/2014/11/17/teaching-history-and-theory-through-popular-culture-my-first-time-designing-a-module/; and James Gunn, "Teaching Science Fiction," *Science Fiction Studies* 23, no. 70 (November 1996), https://www.depauw.edu/sfs/backissues/70/gunn70art.htm.

5. A. Bowdoin Van Riper, *Teaching History with Science Fiction Films* (Lanham, MD: Rowman and Littlefield, 2017).

6. Paul Smith, ed., *The Historian and Film* (New York: Cambridge University Press, 1976).

7. For examples of this debate, see I. F. Clarke, *The Pattern of Expectation, 1644–2001* (London: Cape, 1979), prologue; Roger Luckhurst, *Science Fiction* (Malden, MA: Polity, 2005), part I; and Adam Roberts, *The History of Science Fiction* (New York: Palgrave Macmillan, 2005), chap. 2.

8. Herbert R. Lottman, *Jules Verne: An Exploratory Biography* (New York: St. Martin's Press, 1996), chap. 13.

9. For a discussion of this issue, see Arthur Evans's introduction to Jules Verne, *Invasion of the Sea* (Middletown, CT: Wesleyan University Press, 2001), pp. x–xii. This volume is the first volume in the Wesleyan Classics of Science Fiction series, which is discussed in greater detail in chapter 1.

10. See "A Note on Translation," in Jules Verne, *The Begum's Millions* (Middletown, CT: Wesleyan University Press, 2005), ix.

11. Heather Masri, *Science Fiction: Stories and Contexts* (New York: St. Martin's Press, 2008), 1.

12. Quoted in Gary K. Wolfe, *The Known and the Unknown: The Iconography of Science Fiction* (Kent, OH: Kent State University Press, 1979), 18.

13. Ken MacLeod, The Star Fraction (New York: Tor, 2001).

14. Stites, *Revolutionary Dreams*, 34.

15. Luckhurst, *Science Fiction*, 16.

16. H. G. Wells, *War of the Worlds* (New York: Harper and Brothers, 1898).

SUGGESTED READINGS

Bowler, Peter J. *A History of the Future: Prophets of Progress from H. G. Wells to Isaac Asimov*. New York: Cambridge University Press, 2017.

Luckhurst, Roger. *Science Fiction*. Cambridge, UK: Polity, 2005.

Roberts, Adam. *The History of Science Fiction*. New York: Palgrave Macmillan, 2005.

Stites, Richard. *Revolutionary Dreams: Utopian Vision and Experimental Life in the Russian Revolution*. New York: Oxford University Press, 1989.
Van Riper, A. Bowdoin. *Teaching History with Science Fiction Films*. Lanham, MD: Rowman and Littlefield, 2017.

Chapter 1

Nationalism, Racism, and Imperialism in the Science Fiction of Jules Verne

This chapter describes how instructors can use two of Jules Verne's (1828–1905) novels, *The Begum's Millions* and *Invasion of the Sea*, to engage students with nineteenth-century concepts of nationalism and imperialism.

Classes this lesson can be used for:

- Modern Europe
- World history
- Modern intellectual history
- Imperialism

Science fiction texts:

- Jules Verne, *The Begum's Millions* (1879; Middletown, CT: Wesleyan University Press, 2005)
- Jules Verne, *Invasion of the Sea* (1905; Middletown, CT: Wesleyan University Press, 2001)

As a historical source literature reveals attitudes and aspirations. To use literary sources to unlock the past, it is often useful to move beyond what we today regard as the classics and turn our attention to texts that were popular, or at least commonly available, during the era being studied. Simply put, we must turn our attention to authors and titles that were part of the popular culture of the time, sources that are often forgotten today. I refer to such sources as noncanonical texts.

How can such a noncanonical, or forgotten, text be so useful for teaching? We must first take cognizance that what is considered a classic in our age was not necessarily what people were reading at the time. In his now-classic work on what the French were reading prior to 1789, Robert Darnton makes an important point about history and literature:

> We envisage the literature of every century as a corpus of works grouped around a core of classics; and we derive our notion of the classics from our professors, who took it from their professors, who got it from theirs, and so on, back to some disappearing point in the early nineteenth century. Literary history is an artifice, pieced together over many generations, shortened here and lengthened there, worn thin in some places, patched over in others, and laced through everywhere with anachronism. It bears little relation to the actual experience of literature in the past.[1]

In fact, what eventually becomes the accepted literary canon is usually part of a negotiation of sorts between the present and the past. After all, Melville's *Moby Dick* (1851) was a commercial and critical flop in Antebellum America and did not become canonical literature until the 1920s. The moral of the story? Noncanonical text can be a valuable source for teaching history. By introducing students to what was being read instead of what later generations regard as a classic, we fulfill the historian's job of returning to the primary sources.

For the instructor using science fiction texts to teach history, there are fortunately many such examples of noncanonical texts that can illuminate significant historical subjects—which brings us to work of Jules Verne (1828–1905), an icon of literary history. Born in Nantes, the scion of a bourgeois family, Verne lived through some of the most tumultuous events of nineteenth-century France: The Revolution of 1848, the reign of Napoleon III (1852–1870), the Franco-Prussian War (1870–1871), the Paris Commune (1871), and the creation of the French Empire in Africa and Southeast Asia. Not surprisingly, these events, or the fallout from them, periodically appear in his stories.[2]

According to Arthur Evans, Verne was instrumental in popularizing a new form of literature, one that "mixed fiction with real science."[3] Indeed, when he lived in Paris, Verne spent numerous hours in the Bibliotheque Nationale reading about the latest scientific discoveries and keeping abreast of contemporary events.[4]

Literary historian Adam Roberts argues that, while many of Verne's stories are more accurately classified as adventure, he was also an influential figure in the evolution of science fiction. In fact, Verne was important for establishing the idea that technological extrapolations needed to be realistic.[5] For example, when depicting new types of artillery in his novel *The Begum's Millions*, Verne based his ideas on an extensive study of military innovation, thereby making the imagery plausible. It's fair to say that one of the reasons Verne's stories were popular and remain popular is that they were often believable.[6]

Some of Verne's work—*20,000 Leagues under the Sea* and *Around the World in Eighty Days* come to mind—fit into the literary canon of nineteenth-century France as well as modern science fiction. But it is also true that many of his other novels are less well known today, are just as illustrative of the tumultuous politics and international affairs of his day, and therefore fit into the noncanonical text category.

This chapter focuses on *The Begum's Millions* and *Invasion of the Sea*, which provide insight into two of the most powerful forces in modern world history: nationalism and imperialism. Fortunately for the instructor, new and more accurate translations into English were recently completed and published as part of the Early Classics of Science Fiction series of Wesleyan University Press.

The background to *The Begum's Millions* is an interesting tale. Indeed, the original story on which the novel was based was written immediately after the end of the Franco-Prussian War; that brief conflict not only led to the establishment of a unified Germany, but it was also one of the quintessential stories of modern nationalist rivalries. The first draft of the story that eventually became *The Begum's Millions* was not written by Jules Verne but by Paschal Grousset (1844–1909), who used the pen name Andre Laurie. Grousset wrote the story while he was in exile, having fled France after the fall of the Paris Commune, the short-lived revolutionary government that held power in the French capital briefly after the end of the Franco-Prussian War.[7] The manuscript was submitted to Jules Hetzel, the publisher of Verne's Extraordinary Voyages series, and while Hetzel thought the story had potential, he also believed it needed more revisions than Grousset could provide. As Verne was one of Hetzel's leading authors (and one suspects the most lucrative financially), he arranged for Verne to handle the revisions and for that revised story to be published under Verne's name.[8]

The Begum's Millions is the tale of two men who inherit an immense fortune from a distant relative in India.[9] Frenchman Dr. François Sarrasin is a proponent of modern scientific hygiene, while Professor Schultze is a representation of the latest industrial technology. The basic story line of *The Begum's Millions* can be summarized as a good Frenchman creates a utopia as he squares off against a bad German, who creates a dystopia.[10] Both men take their inheritance and establish colonies in the Pacific Northwest of the United States, where they create different versions of a model city. Dr. Sarrasin's creation of France-Ville is usually regarded by scholars as a utopian community, where clean homes, balanced diets, and broad streets are earmarks of the sanitary, or "hygienic," lifestyle championed by the French physician.

Meanwhile Professor Schultze goes about constructing the military dystopia of Stahlstadt (Steel Town), characterized by rigid mechanization and ruthless order, all apparently for the express purpose of destroying the neighboring utopia by using poison gas dispersed via shells shot out of giant cannons.

Verne spends a great deal of time describing the production of the giant cannon, with particular attention to the plight of the workers. Professor Schultze's ultimate goal: "The destruction of all nations refusing the blend themselves with the German people and reunited with the Fatherland."[11] What the US government thinks of transplanting the Franco-German antagonism to American shores in not addressed in the novel.

Roberts argues that the story is a "crude piece of wish fulfillment," as the inevitable denouncement of Steel Town occurs when Professor Schultze, apparently through a monumental mathematical error in his ballistics calculations, overshoots the French city and sends one of his poison gas shells into orbit.[12] Shortly thereafter, one of Sarrasin's spies infiltrates Schultze's bunker, only to discover that the dictator of Steel Town was killed when one of his own gas shells accidentally ruptured.

As with most literary sources, the student will likely need help from the instructor to comprehend some contemporary references. For example, Professor Schultze is based on German manufacturer Alfred Krupp, who in the nineteenth century was called by some the "Cannon King"; in the novel, Professor Schultze is called the "Steel King." In addition to linkages with prominent historical figures, the novel can easily lend itself to a discussion of national stereotypes, the most obvious being the imagery of the militaristic Germans.[13]

Scholarly analysis of *The Begum's Millions* largely focuses on a few specific subjects, some of which can be used in class. For example, the novel describes the use of gas shells, incendiary bombs, and the potential destructive power of long-range artillery bombardment on cities. As such, the story is an example of Verne's ability to accurately forecast future trends in warfare. Verne's image of the rise of a totalitarian state, in this case epitomized by German militarism, not only can be seen as a reaction to France's recent military defeat but also is a frightening prognostication that turns out to be all too accurate.

Another scholarly approach is to compare and contrast utopian and dystopian societies as created by the industrial age. Both cities contain elements of nineteenth-century life: the effort to create a healthy urban space juxtaposed with the challenges of industrial-scale pollution, for example, can be used as a starting point of a discussion of the romanticization of a simpler, easier, and cleaner preindustrial past. Even with the victory of the French, this is not a feel-good story with a happy ending. Verne was normally a proponent of progress; however, this story lacks the usual Vernian sense of optimism about the future.

One area that has not received a great deal of scholarly attention is the hygienic concept underpinning Dr. Sarrasin's utopian project. While the crude, polluted industrial city, with its time-clock precision in factory production, vividly illustrates the underside of the Industrial Revolution, the life of the residents of France-Ville is also regimented, where contemporary concepts of health and beauty are mandated for the citizens. To put it another way, in Sarrasin's structured society, you have no choice but to be healthy.

Furthermore, France-Ville itself is built by Chinese laborers expressly imported for the job. Verne refers to the anti-Chinese sentiment prevalent in the western United States, and rather than see the "coolies" deported or victims of racial violence, Sarrasin hires them to build his city. Although paid room and board while France-Ville is under construction, the laborers' wages are deposited into the Bank of San Francisco, and upon completion of the project, "each coolie in cashing [their wages] had to promise not to return."[14] So, the workers who built utopia are then denied permission to live in the model city. It can be an informative and difficult discussion to have students consider that the desire to create not just a sanitized world but also a racial utopia is not a historical phenomenon unique to Nazi Germany.

SCIENCE FICTION AND IMPERIALISM

It is easy to characterize Verne's *Invasion of the Sea*, which is set in French North Africa, as just another panegyric to the self-proclaimed civilizing mission of Europeans, whose condescending attitude toward people of color is immortalized in Rudyard Kipling's "The White Man's Burden" (1899). Yet *Invasion of the Sea*, which is the last of the Extraordinary Adventure series published during Verne's lifetime, is also a valuable source for understanding not just the racialist attitudes of European imperialism but also some aspects of its environmental history. For perhaps more than most of his other novels, *Invasion of the Sea* demonstrates Verne's fascination with world geography, scientific investigation, and the grand designs of imperialism to change the natural world.

As stated earlier, one of the reasons that Verne's stories were believable is that he spent a great deal of time in research. In addition to hours spent in libraries reading the latest scientific and cartographical information, Verne also kept notes on contemporary events. He was an avid seaman and traveled extensively, which helped him develop a firsthand perspective on locations for his stories.

Verne based this novel on geographic information he compiled over many years. For example, as early as 1874, a report to the French Geographical Society speculated that the Saharan Basin was once an inland ocean. The author, a captain in the French Army, was also the first to consider a plan to build a canal from the Mediterranean Sea and flood the desert. The result would be a more benign climate, improving communication and travel, thereby making the region more suitable to commerce and modernization. It would also serve as a barrier to the tribes of brigands who preyed on trade.

The novel, set in the 1930s, follows the exploits of Frenchman Captain Hardigan, who is tasked with protecting the engineers as they survey the route the canal will take. Along the way, the protagonists discuss the environmental history of the region, including the assertion that an underground lake continues to exist. While concerned about the long-term effects of their plans, one of the engineers sums up their goal in classic imperialist fashion when he proclaims that he will be satisfied "with bringing this splendid Sahara Sea project to completion."[15]

In addition to protecting the survey team, Hardigan is searching for an escaped brigand, for the adversaries of the French project are a group of Islamic fundamentalist Tuareg Berbers who seek to derail the project. Verne's storyline therefore sets up the basic dichotomy of imperialism: The French represent the forces of modernity who want to improve the Sahara by making it a gateway for trade, which will coincidentally improve France's military position in North Africa. The Berbers, meanwhile, represent the primitive natives who, in their backwardness, are not good stewards of the natural world. Verne shows no sympathy for the Berbers' fear of the destruction of their way of life.

An interesting scene whose significance can easily be missed occurs when the survey party stops to rest in a local community. The *spahis* (native troops) are billeted with Arab families, while the French officers and engineers lodge with one of the colonists. Interestingly, in this scene, Verne captures a part of the French imperialist worldview that continued until the Algerian War of Independence (1954–1962), whereby even after multiple generations, the descendants of the original settlers, who made up 20–25 percent of the population, still referred to themselves as settlers or colonials.

As for the canal project, the culmination of the fight between the French and Berbers is resolved when an earthquake not only finishes the canal but also extends the proposed inland sea even further than the French planned. Like the German plan to build a Berlin-to-Baghdad railroad, the notion of flooding the desert was, as historian Sean McMeekin, points out, "just the kind of half-mad imperial enterprise *fin de siècle* Europeans excelled in."[16]

For those teachers who are less familiar with the interaction of imperialism and the environmental history of North Africa, the article "Reforestation,

Landscape Conservation, and the Anxieties of Empire in French Colonial Algeria" by Carol Ford provides context for how the French regarded the environment of the region. Ford convincingly maintains that French imperialists argued that the natural world contained great potential for world markets and that resources were being wasted by the indigenous population. Not being good stewards of the land was one of the many justifications used by imperial powers to pillage nature in Africa and Asia in the modern world.[17] While the challenge of using *Invasion of the Sea* for class is that the storyline is rather conventional, the historical context can make for some interesting classroom discussion. Indeed, including this novel as part of the study of nineteenth-century nationalism fits easily into the student learning outcomes of most courses in European and world history.

CLASS QUESTIONS AND EXERCISES

After reading *The Begum's Millions*, answer the following questions:

1. Identify the historical context in which Verne wrote the novel (e.g., Was it before or after the Franco-Prussian War of 1870–1871?). Then identify and explain how Verne uses national or ethnic stereotypes for his characters.
2. Compare and contrast the two model communities that are established in the Pacific Northwest. What are the stated goals of each community, and do the ideologies behind the planned communities link to the national stereotypes?
3. What are the fates of each of each group? Does this tell us anything about how nineteenth-century European intellectuals saw utopian projects?

Along with Verne's *Invasion of the Sea*, assign students Carol Ford's "Reforestation, Landscape Conservation, and the Anxieties of Empire in French Colonial Algeria."[18] After reading the article and the book, ask students to answer the following questions:

1. Describe the French attitude to the indigenous population and environment of their North African empire as described in Ford's article (e.g., Was nature likened to an enemy to be tamed?).
2. According to the Verne story, what was the purpose of creating the inland sea?
3. Does the fictional story Verne tells reflect the reality of French attitudes toward nature in their African empire? Use specific examples.

4. Does the Verne story have any resonance with issues we face in our own time?

NOTES

1. Robert Darnton, *The Forbidden Best-Sellers of Pre-Revolutionary France* (New York: W. W. Norton, 1995), xvii.

2. For biographical information, I use Herbert R. Lottman, *Jules Verne: An Exploratory Biography* (New York: St. Martin's Press, 1997), as well as biographical sketches included in some of the texts used in this chapter.

3. Arthur B. Evans, introduction to *Invasion of the Sea* by Jules Verne (Middletown, CT: Wesleyan University Press, 2001), viii.

4. Ibid., 253.

5. Adam Roberts, *The History of Science Fiction* (New York: Palgrave Macmillan, 2005), 129–30.

6. See Evans, introduction, viii.

7. Herbert R. Lottman, *Jules Verne: An Exploratory Biography* (New York: St. Martin's Press, 1997), 216.

8. Ibid., 217.

9. Roberts's argument is based on Hindustani for *queen* or *lady of high rank*. Roberts, *History of Science Fiction*, 139.

10. During class discussion about the novel, one of my students referred to it as a form of "revenge porn."

11. Jules Verne, *The Begum's Millions* (1879; Middletown, CT: Wesleyan University Press, 2005), 47.

12. Roberts, *History of Science Fiction*, 139.

13. See Lottman, *Jules Verne*, 218, for discussion of the stereotypes.

14. Verne, *Begum's Millions*, 120.

15. Jules Verne, *Invasion of the Sea* (1905; Middletown, CT: Wesleyan University Press, 2001), 76.

16. Sean McMeekin, *The Berlin-Baghdad Express: The Ottoman Empire and Germany's Bid for World Power* (Cambridge, MA: Harvard University Press, 2012), 34.

17. Carol Ford, "Reforestation, Landscape Conservation, and the Anxieties of Empire in French Colonial Algeria," *American Historical Review* 113, no. 2 (April 2008): 341–62. Also see her longer monograph on the subject, *Natural Interests: The Contest over Environment in Modern France* (Cambridge, MA: Harvard University Press, 2016).

18. Ford, "Reforestation, Landscape Conservation."

SUGGESTED READING

Ford, Carol. "Reforestation, Landscape Conservation, and the Anxieties of Empire in French Colonial Algeria." *American Historical Review* 113, no. 2 (April 2008): 341–62.

Lottman, Herbert R. *Jules Verne: An Exploratory Biography*. New York: St. Martin's Press, 1997.

McMeekin, Sean. *The Berlin-Baghdad Express: The Ottoman Empire and Germany's Bid for World Power*. Cambridge, MA: Harvard University Press, 2012.

Chapter 2

Invaders from the Red Planet to We're the Martians Now

War of the Worlds in a Variety of Incarnations

This chapter discusses how H. G. Wells's original *War of the Worlds* can be used in class and how it became the progenitor of an entire genre of Martian stories. The chapter also analyzes the significance of the literary Mars and how it can be integrated into class.

Classes this lesson can be used for:

- Modern world history
- US history
- Modern European history
- Introduction to historical thinking

Science fiction films and texts:

- Stephen Baxter, *The Massacre of Mankind: The Sequel to* The War of the Worlds (New York: Crown, 2017)
- *Five Million Years to Earth*, directed by Roy Ward Baker, written by Nigel Kneale (Hammer Films, 1967), https://archive.org/details/quatermassandthepit_202002
- Garret P. Serviss, *Edison's Conquest of Mars* (Los Angeles: Carcosa House, 1947)
- H. G. Wells, *The War of the Worlds* (New York: Harper and Brothers, 1898)

H. G. Wells's *War of the Worlds* is one of the most influential science fiction texts of all time.[1] In addition to the original story, which has remained in print since 1898, a number of authors used Wells's themes to write follow-up stories, from Garret P. Serviss's *Edison's Conquest of Mars* to Stephen Baxter's *The Massacre of Mankind*, a sequel authorized by the Wells estate.[2] A classic comic book version based on the original story was published in 1950.[3] Marvel Comics also used its Amazing Adventures brand for a three-year *War of the Worlds* series that features a character named Killraven who leads the human resistance against a second Martian invasion of Earth a century after the first attempt at occupation flopped.[4]

A preliminary survey of cinematic productions based on the Wells story includes three theatrical movies (in 1953, 2005, and 2023) and at least seven direct-to-video versions, along with two television series. The first TV series on Fox lasted from 1988 to 1990 and billed itself as a sequel to the 1953 movie, while another adaptation ran from 2019 to 2022 and employs the original name and alien invasion theme but substitutes a different alien race for the Martians. In addition, some films, such as the 1998 big-budget production *Independence Day*, are contemporary rewritings of the original story. In this case, it is a computer virus rather than a natural virus that is instrumental in destroying the aliens.

The television shows that contain *War of the World* references or use its themes number in the dozens, including the *Simpsons*' "Treehouse of Horrors XVII" (2006). Finally, there's been at least one musical adaptation, Jeff Wayne's *War of the Worlds* (1978), and at least sixteen radio versions produced. Since the appearance of the 1975 TV movie *The Night That Panicked America*, Orson Welles's 1938 broadcast, the most famous, has cemented itself into American popular culture as an example of popular hysteria over the invasion theme.[5]

The volume and variety of *War of the Worlds* stories and potential subject matter raise an interesting question: how can they be used by the history teacher? To understand the popularity of the Wells storyline, we must first acknowledge its protean character. Simply put, the story was, and likely will continue to be, reworked to fit whatever context the author or producers wanted it to serve. The original text is often interpreted as a critique of imperialism, while some rewrites take an opposite stance. Meanwhile, such versions as the *Simpsons* parody might be seen as criticism of the popular delusions of crowds.

Why the story is so easily adapted requires that we first look at backstory, particularly the role of Mars in modern popular culture. In the modern world, there are in fact two planets named Mars: one is the real fourth planet of our solar system, while the other is the mythical planet of the science fiction genre. In the late nineteenth century, however, the real and mythical Mars were not yet separated, in large part due to the work of Percival Lowell (1855–1916). Lowell was an American entrepreneur in both business and astronomy, whose chief claim to fame was the popularization of the notion that Mars was crisscrossed by artificial canals. Thus, Lowell argued, Mars was almost certainly inhabited. Lowell's publications unleashed a virtual torrent of speculations about the Red Planet, and it became a popular subject for the nascent science fiction genre, replacing the Moon as the preferred destination of interplanetary stories.[6]

By the dawn of the twentieth century, the literary Mars became a source of projection for authors, a place to make commentaries on the human condition. For example, in 1908, Alexander Bogdanov published his novel *Red Star: The First Bolshevik Utopia*, which portrays the type of socialist utopia the author dreamed of establishing on Earth.[7] This tradition continues into the late twentieth century, when science fiction author Kim Stanley Robinson, whose work often reflects his concerns over the environment, published his Mars trilogy—*Red Mars* (1992), *Green Mars* (1993), and *Blue Mars* (1996)—whereby terraforming the planet is used to make commentaries on contemporary political and social issues in the late-twentieth-century United States.

THE ORIGINAL STORY: A CRITIQUE OF IMPERIALISM

The literary Mars not only serves as a place for the utopian adventure, but it can also serve as a grim tale. A theory popular in the nineteenth century was that Mars was much older than the Earth, and Wells uses this concept early in his story to set the stage for the invasion by asserting that the planet seemed to be growing colder as Earthmen watched it through their telescopes. If it was inhabited and it was dying, then its denizens were doomed to a slow death.[8] It is this idea that helped inspire Wells to consider a storyline about an alien race looking at Earth with "envious eyes."

Literary historian Robert Crossley argues that Wells revolutionized the Mars genre by having the Martians invade Earth, a role reversal that marked the "end of human hegemony" in the universe.[9] This new form and plot are apparent from the very beginning of the story, as humans are moved from the lords of creation to the subjects of study by a more advanced race. As Wells's opening paragraph reveals,

> No one would have believed in the last years of the nineteenth century that this world was being watched keenly and closely by intelligences greater than man's and yet as mortal as his own; that as men busied themselves about their various concerns they were scrutinised and studied, perhaps almost as narrowly as a man with a microscope might scrutinise the transient creatures that swarm and multiply in a drop of water . . . No one gave a thought to the older worlds of

space as sources of human danger, or thought of them only to dismiss the idea of life upon them as impossible or improbable. It is curious to recall some of the mental habits of those departed days. At most terrestrial men fancied there might be other men upon Mars, perhaps inferior to themselves and ready to welcome a missionary enterprise. Yet across the gulf of space, minds that are to our minds as ours are to those of the beasts that perish, intellects vast and cool and unsympathetic, regarded this earth with envious eyes, and slowly and surely drew their plans against us. And early in the twentieth century came the great disillusionment.[10]

For the instructor seeking to use the original Wells story, the parallels to European imperialism become more obvious as one moves through the novel. For example, Wells refers to the destruction of the indigenous people of Tasmania to provide a reference point for the Martians' motivation. Furthermore, Wells studied biology and evolution under T. H. Huxley and was cognizant of the various African and Asian diseases that were often fatal to European imperialists.[11]

It is important that the plotline of the original story not be confused with later film versions. The original story is told from two different perspectives: an unnamed journalist who witnesses the Martians arrival in Surrey and details the early battles with the British Army and the journalist's younger brother (also unnamed), who tells the story of the destruction of London. In the second half of the novel, the journalist describes the Martian occupation of England, their use of poison gas as a weapon, and the feeding on human blood to regenerate themselves, for it turns out the Martians are as decrepit as their home planet. Wells biographer David Smith points out that the author's attention to the setting of the English countryside was so precise that "with the early version of the Ordnance Survey maps it is still possible to follow exactly where the Martians went."[12]

In addition to providing a critique of imperialism, Wells targets human vanity, especially the hubris of fin-de-siecle European belief in their technological dominance. Although the invaders suffer casualties, the Martians quickly demonstrate their technological superiority over mankind.[13] Furthermore, in the end it is not human ingenuity that destroys the aliens:

> For so it had come about, as indeed I and many men might have foreseen had not terror and disaster blinded our minds. These germs of disease have taken toll of humanity since the beginning of things—taken toll of our prehuman ancestors since life began here. But by virtue of this natural selection of our kind we have developed resisting power; to no germs do we succumb without a struggle, and to many—those that cause putrefaction in dead matter, for instance—our living frames are altogether immune. But there are no bacteria in Mars, and directly

these invaders arrived, directly they drank and fed, our microscopic allies began to work their overthrow. Already when I watched them they were irrevocably doomed, dying and rotting even as they went to and fro. It was inevitable. By the toll of a billion deaths man has bought his birthright of the earth, and it is his against all comers; it would still be his were the Martians ten times as mighty as they are. For neither do men live nor die in vain.[14]

Perhaps one of the most remarkable things about Wells's story is how it spread and inspired both pirated versions and rewrites. Indeed, shortly after it was published in serial form in *Pearson's Magazine* (1897) and even before the first edition of the book was published in 1898, two US newspapers revised the story, with the title *Fighters from Mars*. The *New York Evening World* reset the story as an attack on New York City, while the *Boston Post* did a similar rewrite in order for the Martians to destroy New England.[15] The tradition of rewriting parts of the story to have different epicenters of human civilization be the target is perhaps one of the reasons the story remains popular. In each rewrite, the location of the Martian invasion, whether it be Washington, DC, or Tokyo, not only reveals the cultural biases (perhaps verging on ethnocentrism) but also personalizes the story for the potential reader. Such geographic transitions are also found in later cinematic versions of the story.

THE PRO-IMPERIALIST SEQUEL: THE HERO-SCIENTIST AND CASUAL GENOCIDE

Garrett Putnam Serviss (1851–1929) was a journalist, astronomer, and popularizer of scientific subjects. The ink was barely dry on the serialized and heavily modified *Fighters from Mars*, when Serviss's unauthorized sequel to the unauthorized story began to appear, again in serial form, in 1898. Interestingly *Edison's Conquest of Mars* was not published in book form until 1947, but it remains in print.[16]

Where Wells depicts humanity as being humbled, indeed humiliated, by the Martians' sophistication, Serviss's story returns humanity to the top of the interplanetary hierarchy. Fearing that the Martians are planning a second invasion, world leaders commission Thomas Edison and other prominent Anglophone scientists to study Martian technology as a means of taking the fight to the enemy. Edison, the quintessential hero-scientist, improves the Martians' technology by constructing spaceships powered by "repulsor rays" and a "disintegrator" (ray) gun.

Powered by this new technology, the human fleet begins the counterattack on Mars. Like the Martian invaders of Earth, Edison's fleet suffers losses in heavy fighting; however, they do take two prisoners. The first is a Martian who teaches them the language of the Red Planet, while the second is a human, Aina, the last remnant of a slave population taken from Kashmir more than nine thousand years ago. It seems the Martians had visited Earth in ancient times, although in this earlier expedition, they stopped only long enough to take slaves and build the pyramids. In fact, the Great Sphinx is an image of the Martian ruler.

Aina informs Edison that the Martian cities are all below sea level, and by destroying the dam at Mars's north pole, the earthlings can wipe out 90 percent of the Martian population before they return triumphant to Earth. Although Serviss's story is certainly an example of hack literature, it is also an example of the pro-imperialist vision of the United States in the late nineteenth century. Indeed, the story appeared concomitantly with the Spanish-American War and the beginnings of the United States as a global power. Thus, Mars in this case serves as a replacement for American aspirations for conquest.[17]

"WE'RE THE MARTIANS NOW": A POST-HOLOCAUST VERSION OF THE MARTIAN INVASION STORY

Five Million Years to Earth (alternate title: *Quatermass and the Pit*), a 1967 British sci-fi/horror film, might at first seem an unlikely example of the Wellsian story genre adapted to contemporary issues.[18] The film is one of several British TV and big-screen productions to feature the character Professor Bernard Quatermass. Quatermass is an example of the hero-scientist, but unlike Serviss's Edison, this British counterpart has a conscience.

Screenwriter/producer Nigel Kneale, who created the Quatermass character, is credited with also developing some of the earliest post-1945 science fiction serials on British television: *The Quatermass Experiment* (1953), *Quatermass II* (1955), and *Quatermass and the Pit* (1958–1959). According to his obituary, "Kneale dealt in terror—a world that seemed ever on the verge of collapse into appalling, awesome chaos." Meanwhile, in an oft-repeated story, his TV productions were said to "empty the pubs," as people stayed home to watch.[19]

Quatermass and the Pit is credited with "melding science fiction and horror," and the 1967 big-screen remake (released as *Five Million Years to Earth*) was "one of the best ever Hammer productions and was enormously influential in the United States, especially to horror-film-makers like John Carpenter."[20] In addition to being easier to use in the classroom due to its length, being just longer than ninety minutes, compared to the multipart TV series from 1958–1959, it is also more easily accessible through streaming.[21]

The story begins when workers on an extension of the London Underground discover the skeletal remains of five-million-year-old primates alongside an alien spaceship. Professor Quatermass teams up with Natural History Museum director Roney to investigate the link between the primate remains and the ship, despite fierce opposition to their research from a skeptical military official and the civil administration.

As the search for answers progresses, the bodies of arthropods in the ship are uncovered. Their size and structure indicate they came from a low-gravity, low-oxygen world, and Professor Quatermass wonders "if they can be Martians." When it is pointed out that Mars is a dead world, Quatermass retorts, "Perhaps a world that's dead now but a few million years ago [might have been] teeming with life." The film, therefore, embraces the theory that Mars is a much older world than Earth and is in the Wellsian tradition that a dying world and a dying race looked to their neighboring planet for salvation.

Quatermass then asks Roney, "If we found that our Earth was doomed, say by climatic changes, what would we do about it?"

Roney responds, "Nothing. Just go on squabbling as usual."

A cynical response? Perhaps, but to our own age that is experiencing the threat of climate change and widespread climate change denial, it was an accurate prediction.

Using advanced technology that enables Roney and Quatermass to access deep recesses of the human brain, they unlock a "race memory" from the mind of one of their team members that shows of life on Mars five million years ago. The Martians, who resemble the horned devils of human nightmares, were engaged in what Quatermass calls a "race purge" and "ritual slaughter," the goal of which was to destroy any mutations and maintain a fixed society.

Their world dying, these Martians looked to Earth, as previous invaders did, although in this case, the invasion happened five million years ago. The arthropod Martians, however, were unable to survive Earth's atmosphere or endure the heavier gravity. Thus, they experimented on primates to direct evolution in a specific direction and create a surrogate species—colonization by proxy, as it were—and implanted in the evolving human genetic pattern subservience to the Martian ideals of a fixed society that must destroy all those who stand outside the collective.

Later in the film, as the Martian ship activates from its long-dormant state, it begins to take over the mind of Londoners, including briefly Quatermass. As an energy image of a Martian—looking like the horned devil of legend—is projected above the city, the humans, now neo-Martians, begin to kill all those who are not part of the collective mind. Quatermass himself manages to shake off the mind control and tells Roney that he wanted to kill him because he was "different."

What, then, defeats this Martian invasion? Not a microbe but the laws of physics. As the Martian energy field hovers over the city, Roney hits upon the answer: "Mass into energy. The fundamental law. The Devil's enemy was iron . . . It's what they'd never allow for, even that scrap of knowledge in minds that were free to use it." Roney then sacrifices himself by driving a metal crane into the Martian energy field, literally short-circuiting the invasion. Once again, the Martian invasion is thwarted not by military might but by the simple law of physics.

As with all science fiction texts and film, the first step in determining how the instructor can take advantage of this film in class is to place it in proper historical context. Certainly, the film is an example of the Martian-invasion genre. Yet it is also a product of the post-Holocaust era. In 1898, for example, the hero-scientist character commits a genocide of the Martians with barely concealed glee. Fast-forward to 1967, and Qartermass serves as the conscience of the world; his disdain for the military authorities fits into the rebellious nature of 1960s politics. Unlike Serviss's Edison, Quatermass prevents mass slaughter, in this case of all those who resist incorporation into the Martian hive. The references to race purges and the desire to "cleanse" the colony of those who do not fit into the collective are also clear examples of the legacy of World War II.

CLASS QUESTIONS AND EXERCISES

Read H. G. Wells, *War of the Worlds*, and then answer the following questions:

1. How is this novel a critique of imperialism? Provide at least three examples from the text to justify your argument.
2. Explain the significance of the parson and the artilleryman to the story. What themes or ideas in British history do you think they represent?

Read Garret Serviss, *Edison's Conquest of Mars*, and Steven Mollmann, "The *War of the Worlds* in the *Boston Post* and the Rise of American Imperialism: 'Let Mars Fire,'" and answer the following questions:

1. How is the Serviss novel an example of pro-imperialist literature?
2. Analyze the role of hero-scientist Edison in the story.

A longer project for students can be as follows:

1. What role does Mars play in the popular imagination?

2. Take each decade from 1960 to the present, and locate at least one example in film or literature of a Martian-invasion story. Then compare and contrast them with the genre established by Wells in his original novel.

NOTES

1. For the literary context of Wells's work, see Adam Roberts, *H. G. Wells: A Literary Life* (New York: Palgrave Macmillan, 2019).

2. Stephen Baxter, *The Massacre of Mankind: The Sequel to* War of the Worlds (New York: Crown, 2017).

3. "*War of the Worlds* by H. G. Wells," *Classics Illustrated*, no. 124 (January 1955), https://archive.org/details/WarOfTheWorldsClassic1955.

4. Also published as a collection. See Donald McGregor, with Roy Thomas, Gerry Conway, Marv Wolfman, and Bill Mantlo, *Killraven: Warrior of the Worlds*, vol. 1, *1973–1983* (New York: Marvel Worldwide, 2021).

5. There is some doubt that the broadcast caused a major panic, as the listening audience numbered about 12 million, and it is estimated that about 1 in 12 thought the attack was real. The postbroadcast story may very well be an example of creating a historical incident that really didn't happen. Mark Memmott, "75 Years Ago, 'War of the Worlds' Started a Panic. Or Did It?" NPR, October 30, 2013, https://www.npr.org/sections/thetwo-way/2013/10/30/241797346/75-years-ago-war-of-the-worlds-started-a-panic-or-did-it.

6. See Robert Crossley, *Imagining Mars: A Literary History* (Middletown, CT: Wesleyan University Press, 2011), chap. 4.

7. See the modern translation of his novels in Alexander Bogdanov, *Red Star: The First Bolshevik Utopia*, ed. Loren R. Graham and Richard Stites, trans. Charles Rougle (Bloomington: Indiana University Press, 1984).

8. On the theory that Mars was older than Earth, see Crossley, *Imagining Mars*, 19; for a discussion of Wells and the writing of *War of the Worlds*, see David C. Smith, *H. G. Wells: Desperately Mortal* (New Haven, CT: Yale University Press, 1986), 64–67.

9. Crossley, *Imagining Mars*, 110.

10. H. G. Wells, *War of the Worlds* (New York: Harper and Brothers, 1898), 1–2.

11. Crossley, *Imaging Mars*, 117; Smith, Wells: *Desperately Mortal*, 10–16.

12. Smith, *H. G. Wells*, 65.

13. Crossley, *Imagining Mars*, 117.

14. Wells, *War of the Worlds*, 282–83.

15. See Steven Mollmann, "*The War of the Worlds* in the *Boston Post* and the Rise of American Imperialism: 'Let Mars Fire,'" *English Literature in Transition* 53, no. 4 (2010): 387–412.

16. Crossley, *Imagining Mars*, 124. *Edison's Conquest of Mars* can be read in its entirety at Project Gutenberg, https://www.gutenberg.org/files/19141/19141-h/19141-h.htm.

17. Crossley, *Imagining Mars*, 125; H. Bruce Lincoln, *War Stars: The Superweapon and the American Imagination* (New York: Oxford University Press, 1988), 67.

18. Peter Hutchings, "'We're the Martians Now': British Invasion Fantasies of the 1950s and 19 60s," in *British Science Fiction Cinema*, ed. I. Q. Hunter (New York: Routledge, 1999), 33–47, discusses the Quatermass genre.

19. Jack Adrian, "Nigel Kneale: Creator of Quatermass," *Independent*, November 2, 2006, http://news.independent.co.uk/people/obituaries/article1948184.ece.

20. Adrian, "Nigel Kneale."

21. *Five Million Years to Earth*, dir. Roy Ward Baker, writ. Nigel Kneale (Hammer Films, 1967), https://archive.org/details/quatermassandthepit_202002.

SUGGESTED READING

Crossley, Robert. *Imagining Mars: A Literary History*. Middletown, CT: Wesleyan University Press, 2011.

Hutchings, Peter. "'We're the Martians Now': British Invasion Fantasies of the 1950s and 1960s." In *British Science Fiction Cinema*, edited by I. Q. Hunter. New York: Routledge, 1999.

Lincoln, H. Bruce. *War Stars: The Superweapon and the American Imagination*. New York: Oxford University Press, 1988.

Chapter 3

Things to Come

The Fall and Rise of Civilization in the Future War

In this chapter I show how technological change helped inspire a new type of tale, the future-war story, and how it can provide insight into the anxieties of the modern age.

Classes this lesson can be used for:

- Modern US history
- Twentieth-century Europe
- Modern world history
- Modern war history
- Intellectual history
- Introduction to historical thinking

Science fiction films and texts:

- Philip Francis Nowlan, "The Airlords of Han," *Amazing Stories* 3, no. 12 (March 1929): 1106–36
- Philip Francis Nowlan, "Armageddon—2419 A.D.," *Amazing Stories* 3, no. 5 (August 1928): 422–49
- *Things to Come*, directed by William Cameron Menzies, written by H. G. Wells (London Films, 1936)
- H. G. Wells, "The Land Ironclads," *Strand Magazine* (December 1903): 501–2
- H. G. Wells, *The War in the Air*, Bison Frontiers of Imagination (1908; Lincoln: University of Nebraska Press, 2002)

On November 10, 1932 (the day before Armistice Day), former British prime minister Stanley Baldwin made a frightening prophecy: "It is well . . . for the man in the street to realize that there is no power on earth that can protect him from being bombed, whatever people may tell him. The bomber will always get through."[1] The fear of an aerial attack on civilian populations was symptomatic of a prominent anxiety of the post-1918 world, and Baldwin's statement demonstrates how deeply the concern had inculcated itself into political culture. Yet Baldwin's statement that the bomber will always get through had in fact been a staple of science fiction stories for nearly a decade before it entered interwar political discourse. To put it another way, had politics finally caught up to science fiction? In this chapter, I show how H. G. Wells was among the pioneers of the future-war genre and how these stories, such as the film *Things to Come* (1936), can be used in a classroom setting.

Despite the aura of being prophetic, it is interesting to note that science fiction writers before 1914 often failed to understand how the technological revolution of the previous century was transforming warfare. Even those writers who took technological developments into consideration still depicted war as being fought in the old model; indeed, a large percentage of future-war stories concentrated on predicting how decisive battles and heroic individuals would determine the outcome of the action and thereby the course of history.[2] Many authors were also obsessed with the notion that those nations who did not embrace the new technology were doomed to be defeated in a future war. In later years, such stories would be called preparedness novels.[3]

Unlike many of his contemporaries, H. G. Wells understood how technological change would revolutionize warfare. Despite this understanding prior to 1914, he still concluded that a more rapid victory should be easier "in the future even than it had proved in the past."[4] However, Wells was not "entrapped in a dilemma of cause and effect,"[5] unable to assimilate the coming transformation of war. Certainly, Wells plays an important role in the genesis of the twentieth-century variants of the future-war story.

According to I. F. Clarke, Wells wrote the "most remarkable future-war stories in the history of the genre." Wells removed himself from a parochial national perspective to examine the "universal consequences" of the wars to come and matched the new weapons he envisioned with the specific consequences of their use. Wells, who contemplated the rise of the "flying man" as early 1893, was one of only a handful of writers in the early twentieth century who understood that the developing technology of air power would revolutionize both warfare and society in general.[6]

One of Wells's most famous stories, and one that at least one historian argues had a direct effect on military thinking, is his 1903 short story "The Land Ironclads."[7] The story focuses on a war between the "townsmen" and their rural neighbors; while no explanation of the causes of the war is given, the first part of the story is told from the perspective of a correspondent interviewing members of the rural/agrarian side. In a classic use of social-Darwinist rhetoric, the townsmen are described as a "crowd of devitalised townsmen . . . They're clerks, they're factory hands, they're students, they're civilised men. They can write, they can talk, they can make and do all sorts of things, but they're poor amateurs at war."[8]

Wells, however, rejects the notion that urban life leads to a loss of prowess, and the townsmen defeat their opponents with machines resembling ships adapted to land use (hence the story title), which are easily identified by modern readers as prototanks. With that in mind, the most interesting aspect of Wells story is how, at the end, the correspondent still describes the victorious townsmen as something less than men. Wells's story enables the instructor to look at such issues as racialist thought from the perspective of an early-twentieth-century Edwardian, where the social-Darwinist notions of the day, especially the fear of racial degeneration, helped inspire the creation of such organizations as the Boy Scouts.

Wells's 1908 novel *The War in the Air* provides a useful perspective for his sense of the potential shape of modern warfare and clues about how early the story's narrative structure began to develop the basis of his more famous cinematic story *Things to Come* (1936). *The War in the Air* centers around a rather inconsequential Englishman who manages, through his own clumsiness, to become embroiled in a surprise German aerial assault on the United States. The German attack devastates New York City and signals the start of a worldwide war, which in the time of only a few short months destroys urban centers and leads to the breakdown of civilization.

The story ends a number of years after the war winds down, with society stagnating at a very low socioeconomic level and the lead character lamenting, "You can say what you like . . . It didn't ought ever to 'ave begun."[9] As prophetic as the imagery of the potential destruction wrought by aerial bombardment might be, what is perhaps a more intriguing and useful pedagogical tool is the discussion of why Wells believed that civilization would collapse so quickly after such a brief conflict. According to David Smith, Wells was extremely pessimistic about the ability of modern society to meet extraordinary crisis, "either bravely or intelligently." Smith also describes the *War in the Air* as a "strong depiction of Wellsian views on the military future, with relatively little of his message about world government, socialism, or education."[10] With that in mind, *The War in the Air* must also be understood as part of a developing literary and artistic genre that both glamorized and, in some cases, dreaded the advent of the air age.

Interestingly, the main vehicles of aerial destruction were not based on the Wright brothers' mechanism. The inspiration for Wells's apocalyptic vision was the high-profile flights of Count Zeppelin in Germany. The only heavier-than-air machines in the story are in the hands of the Japanese pilots, who prophetically use them as flying samurai. It should come as no surprise that the year immediately following Wells's story witnessed the "Phantom Airship Scare" in England.[11] According to Alfred Gollin, the "Airship Scare" of May 1909, which was characterized by multiple sightings of what looked like Zeppelins over parts of eastern England, was superficially caused by escalating political tensions between Britain and Germany. In addition to the international context, Gollin documents the role of domestic concerns about national security and how political rivalries between the conservative and liberal parties also added fuel to the speculations about possible aerial assault.

The flights of the Zeppelin forcefully hammered home that it was only a matter of time before the channel was crossed by air—which occurred later in 1909—and that Britain could no longer count on its geography to serve as a first line of defense.[12] While the exact relationship between Wells's story and the events of 1909 cannot be determined, the timing is, to say the least, suggestive.

It is important not to interpret the *War in the Air* as a polemical call to arms but rather to focus on what it represents in Wells's intellectual involvement with air power. Such novels as *The War in the Air* and, four years later, *The World Set Free* (1914) were Wells's attempt to synthesize his vision of history and social prophecy in the form of a future-war story. Indeed, according to Frank McConnell,

> The rhythm of history established in *The War in the Air* was to become the permanent rhythm of his utopian histories of the future, the permanent situation he envisioned as necessary to the founding of a world state, the awakening of human beings to their endangered position and their only hope for survival. A massive destruction, bloody, and universal war *must* occur, given the present condition of human venality and short sightedness—a war whose whole-sale disaster is sufficient to return civilization to the primal sociological muck out of which all human communities have so arduously struggled.[13]

Wells always hoped that "men might make a better world" and that the will of the individual could transform the "shabby spectacle of history into something noble and shining."[14]

Of particular interest in this period is the image of the airman. During World War I, thousands of foot soldiers died anonymously every week, killed by artillery or machine-gun fire. The airman, however, became the new romantic hero, the "knight" of the skies, whose exploits were celebrated in wartime propaganda and mourned by the nation when they died in combat. Not surprisingly, the wartime motifs became a fixture of popular culture after the war.[15]

Interwar pulp magazines, such as *Wings*, *Air Trails*, *War Birds*, and *Dare-Devil Aces*, celebrated the exploits of airmen and airpower. Many stories in these magazines are historical fiction or the retelling of stories from the war years.[16] It is therefore not too surprising to discover that one of the legacies of World War I is that the airman also becomes a ubiquitous character, and usually the hero, in science fiction stories.[17]

As Robert Wohl has documented, aviation plays a profound role in popular culture during the twentieth century. The aerial age was more than just the development of flying machines; it also involved the development of an image of flight that permeated Western culture. Flying represented the Western ability to conquer the air and challenge the boundaries of "time, space, and even death." Aviation represented the birth a new man, the aviator, who revitalized society, and the exploits of these men (and their machines) were celebrated in postcards, poetry, all manner of souvenirs, literature, and film.[18]

The aerial age was also a tool of nationalism. In the pre-1914 era, one lesser-known aspect of the arms race between France and Germany was the search for more efficient and powerful means of heavier-than-air flight. Indeed, during the prewar and later wartime, air power became a symbol of national power and prestige.[19] The more successful the airmen and the more technologically advanced their craft, the more invigorating the national ethos seemed.[20]

So, by 1918, it is fair to say that the image of aviation brought together concepts about technology, nationalism, and spectacle. That these trends also coincided with the further consolidation of the science fiction genre is not too surprising, given that the focus of the literature prior to 1918 presaged many postwar trends.

This brings us back to Prime Minister Baldwin's statement, where the fear of the aerial assault had penetrated modern political discourse. Prior to World War I, many intellectuals, including writers of science fiction, regarded war as good; war settled political disputes quickly, and with the social-Darwinist notions of the day, war improved the quality of a nation's racial stock.[21] The belief in a short war that was good for the nation had, however, died on the battlefields of Verdun and the Somme. Mass slaughter and physical destruction challenged conventional methods of describing war, whether as actual conflict or the tale of the war to come. According to I. F. Clarke, science fiction stories that dealt with future-war scenarios "turned from the nationalistic ready-for-anything style" that dominated the pre-1914 era and toward a more pessimistic attitude post-1918.[22]

Depending on which authority you read, World War I either created the modern world (intellectually) or hastened a return to tradition or at least a nostalgia for an imagined past. In his classic work *The Great War and Modern*

Memory, literary critic Paul Fussell argues that World War I had a profound effect on how we describe and remember war, especially using irony and sarcasm to describe military leadership. Modris Ekstein, a cultural historian, argues that the war helped fashion a new Western mindset (especially through the avant-garde) that also changed attitudes toward war. Fussell and Ekstein, for example, look at the classic works of postwar literature, such as Erich Marie Remarque's *All Quiet on the Western Front* and Robert Graves's *Goodbye to All That*.[23]

Jay Winter, meanwhile, asserts that, rather than having created a new vocabulary, the war, or more specifically the aftermath of the war, witnessed a retreat to traditional literary and psychological motifs to explain the wartime experience, especially in trying to find a means of coping with the war's physical desolation and mass casualties. Winter looks at the proliferation of war memorials, remembrance books, and other souvenirs of nostalgia to demonstrate how people sought comfort in traditional methods of memory as a means of making sense of the modern world.[24]

Interestingly, while both schools of thought (sometimes identified by the nicknames "traditional" and "modern") focus in large part on literary texts, neither devotes much attention to science fiction. This is a significant lacuna, for science fiction is simultaneously historic and modern, "one informed by a profound engagement with the most pressing issues of the contemporary world," so an examination of science fiction war stories is useful for understanding the impact of war on the Western psyche.[25]

I. F. Clarke's analysis of future-war stories tends toward acceptance of the modernist thesis, arguing that "after 1918 it was no longer possible to say that war was merely the extension of policy by others means" and claiming that prowar propaganda largely disappeared from future-war stories. Furthermore, Clarke agrees with the assertion that there was a postwar revolt against literary tradition and that after 1918 many of the new generation of writers spoke from experience, having served during the war.[26]

Several years prior to Baldwin's warnings about aerial attack, American journalist Philip Francis Nowlan (1888–1940) created one of the most iconic characters in US science fiction.[27] "Armageddon—2419 A.D." and "The Airlords of Han," published in *Amazing Stories* in August 1928 and March 1929, respectively, mark the first appearance of character Anthony Rogers, later renamed Buck Rogers for a syndicated comic strip. The character is a twentieth-century flyer who was trapped in a mine near Pittsburgh and, thanks to a strange gas, survived in suspended animation into the twenty-fifth century.

The story arc combines the importance of air power with an image of America under the yoke of foreign domination. Nowlan incorporates many of the racial fears and anxieties of America during the interwar years, especially an Asiatic enemy—the Han—attacking and occupying America, an interesting change from the prewar era, when a Eurocentric image of the foreign invader was as likely a scenario.[28]

The story uses several themes familiar to anyone who has read Wells. An aerial attack devastates the United States, causing the collapse of civilization. Being driven from the cities, however, leads to a return not to barbarism for the hardy Americans but rather a form of pastoralism combined with technological innovation, which enables the Americans to form neotribal groups, called "gangs," to fight Han oppression.

Rogers awakens from suspended animation and, using his skills as an aviator from World War I, joins the fight. The neo-American gangs have developed a new material that, when strapped to their backs, enables them to defy gravity (slightly different from flying). Thus bouncing along, the resistance jumps onto tall buildings to kill the insidious Han. The two stories, later combined as the novel *Armageddon 2419 AD*, contain numerous anti-Asian stereotypes that, though possibly disturbing to students, provide an important window into some of the common bigotries of the twentieth-century United States.[29]

The story is told from Rogers's perspective, and he dubs the fight again the Han as America's Second War of Independence. Naturally, Rogers not only is the hero, but he also gets the girl, Wilma Deering, and fitting the with genre, he becomes the leader of the gang, democratizing it as they go on to defeat the Han. Rogers the hero is part of the lionization of the skilled and daring aviators, who use technology to fight against the odds and win.

Bringing the Nowlan stories into a classroom can be a challenge, as the anti-Asian animus can make students uneasy, so it is very important that a proper foundation is set prior to reading the stories. As recommended reading for the instructor, Roger Daniels's *Asian America* not only provides an interpretive framework for the Chinese and Japanese immigrant experience, but it also analyzes the nature of the prejudice these communities faced.[30]

At first glance, the 1936 film *Things to Come* seems to confirm Susan Sontag's dictum that science fiction films are "about disaster rather than science."[31] *Things to Come* is the brainchild of H. G. Wells and émigré producer Alexander Korda, and its inspiration comes from Wells's 1934 novel *The Shape of Things to Come*.[32] Although the visual imagery was fashioned by Korda, the theme, much of the dialogue, and the ultimate message belong to Wells, who was deeply involved in its production, even to the point of recruiting the musical score from Arthur Bliss.[33] In creating his cinematic image of the future, Wells drew upon his understanding of historical development. Indeed, his theme of the rise, decline, fall, and rise of civilization could easily have been written as a history of Europe from Rome until the modern age, albeit compressed into a narrative that sees these events occurring in less than a century.³⁴

The movie begins with the outbreak of the Second Great War at Christmas 1940, which is immediately followed by an aerial bombardment that devastates the city of Everytown (a metaphor for London). That the cinematic images of massive civilian casualties appeared only a few years after Baldwin's assertion about the inevitability of the bomber is no coincidence. What is certainly prophetic, and the instructor would do well to keep this in mind, is that the deep-seated anxieties over the fate of civilians in a future war was not really an exaggeration.³⁵

The war continues over the course of twenty-five years and leads to the breakdown of civilization. With the cessation of hostilities, the survivors must deal with the ravages of a plague (referred to as the "walking sickness") and the return of barbarism. War and pestilence are followed by the establishment of a neofeudal state in Everytown, where a brutal chieftain, called "the Boss" (played by Ralph Richardson), rules and wages an interminable war against neighboring tribes. It seems as if civilization will take centuries to climb out of this pit.

Yet all is not lost, for the denizens of Everytown are saved from the Boss and the ravages of primitivism by a group of technocratic airmen who call themselves "World Communications." Their leader, John Cabal (Raymond Massey), once a resident of Everytown, tells the Boss he is now known as "Wings over the World." After a brief struggle—verbal, mental, and physical—the Boss is overwhelmed by the superior technology of World Communications, and the reign of the airmen begins.

Wells cast the film's story as a series of juxtapositions: between rationalism and obliviousness, between science and barbarism, between the future and reaction/conservatism. For example, on the eve of war, a young John Cabal debates the significance of war to technological progress with a neighbor:

Passworthy: War doesn't stop progress. It stimulates progress.

Cabal: Yes, war's a *highly* stimulating thing. But you can overdo a stimulant. The next dose may be fatal.

Sadly, Cabal is correct, for while the war initially leads to technological progress, it destroys civilization. The symbolic acknowledgment of this destruction comes when a young mechanic attempting to rebuild Everytown's air force in 1968 proclaims, "Flying is over. Everything is over. Civilization is dead."

A short while later, a now-elderly John Cabal meets with some of his friends in the ruins of Everytown and explains the significance of the Boss in contemporary affairs:

Not an unusual type. Everywhere, you see, we find these little semimilitary upstarts robbing, fighting. That is what endless warfare has worked out to—brigandage. What else could happen? And we, who are all that is left of the old engineers and mechanics, are turning our hands to salvage the world. We have the airways, what is left of them; we have the sea. We have ideas in common; the freemasonry of efficiency—the brotherhood of science. We are the natural trustees of civilization [*sic*] when everything else has failed.

Following the Boss's downfall, Cabal and the airmen turn their talents to rebuilding civilization. Extended scenes show New-Age machines digging and building, until we see a new Everytown situated beneath pristine countryside in 2036. A little girl learns from her great-grandfather how this modern age was built, juxtaposing pictures of New York City with modern Everytown.

We learn that John Cabal's grandson Oswald Cabal now heads the ruling council. All of the Earth has been harnessed to serve the world state, which enables its citizens to enjoy prosperity, achieve intellectual stimulation, and extend lives. We also learn that the next great frontier, space, is about to be breached, as a giant space gun is preparing to send a capsule with two occupants around the moon.

Unlimited progress does not sit well with *all* the citizens of Everytown, for even in this utopia, we find a snake in the grass in the shape of the artist Theotocopoulos (Wells describes him as a direct descendant of El Greco). Theotocopoulos despises progress and leads a revolt to destroy the symbol of the new world order, the giant space gun. The conflict between Oswald Cabal and Theotocopoulos, juxtaposing the future of progress with a desire to return to a simpler time, provides the overarching backdrop to the final section of the film. It is the vehicle for Wells's ultimate message. Cabal and the artist each present their case for the space mission, in which Cabal's own daughter will travel.

Although deleted from the final version of the film, Wells sought to demonstrate his arguments through a series of vignettes. In each vignette, Theotocopoulos's words spark a debate about the nature of progress. In one such example, Theotocopoulos appeals to the people, "Make an end to progress now. We are content with the simple, sensuous, limited, loveable life of man, and we want no other. Between the dark past of history and the incalculable future, let us snatch today—and live. What is the future to us? Give the Earth peace, and leave our human lives alone." A group of spelunkers, prospecting several miles underground, listen to the speech on their portable "televisor." They regard the artist as a reactionary, and one worries that the speech will "stir up a lot of lazy people . . . They hate this endless exploration and experimenting."

The question of the space gun develops an important theme for a Wellsian future. Once the Earth has been united in a world state, when human civilization provides everything its inhabitants need, what will prevent entropy from taking its toll? How do you maintain the cutting edge when war itself is conquered? The quest for new frontiers, beneath the Earth and in space, will ensure that humanity will not degenerate.

Despite Theotocopoulos's efforts, the space gun is fired, and the future continues. When asked by his friend Passworthy (whose son is also aboard the capsule), "Is there never to be an age of happiness? Is there never to be rest?" Cabal replies, "Rest enough for the individual man. Too much of it and too soon, and we call it death. But for *man*, no rest and no ending. He must go on—conquest beyond conquest . . . And when he has conquered all the deeps of space and all the mysteries of time—still he will be beginning." The film ends with a challenge to the audience: "Which shall it be?"[36]

Wells's storyline demonstrates that the debates about the shape of future wars were certainly part of the popular consciousness, or at least the cinematic manifestations of popular culture. The film is interesting on several levels, one of which is how it demonstrates the complex interaction of hope and anxiety for the viewer; the hope is the airman saving Western civilization, while the anxiety comes from the imagery of an aerial attack temporarily destroying that civilization. The film also represents a common theme in 1930s future-war fiction: the fear that scientific and technological advances in machines and weapons will lead to an apocalyptic war.

These anxieties were not just expressed in fiction, as military intellectuals engaged in a robust debate about the lessons of World War I, although it took some time for the impact of technology and new machinery to change the attitude of professional military men. For example, in France, Britain, and the United States, military officers initially had not regarded World War I as a watershed in modern conflict. In examining the battlefield lessons from Verdun, the Somme, and the Dardanelles, soldiers often fell back on the conventional wisdom that, in order to win, it was necessary to defeat an opposing field army. As with prewar writers, interwar military thinkers initially emphasized the "cult of the offensive," and the segregation of the military front from civilian affairs (and populations) was considered normal. Little credence was often given to the concept of total war.[37]

The sense that weapons of mass destruction could and would be used in the next war provides an interesting insight into a changing attitude. Although many Americans regard science, scientists, and technology as forces for good, by the 1930s, some American authors began exhibiting ambivalent feelings toward what had been a widespread faith in human progress. Indeed, in the 1930s, the image of technology began to change from being a power for good—stopping war or solving economic problems—to a force that could accelerate the destructive potential of society.[38] Meanwhile, the benevolent scientist/inventor is transformed in some stories into the mad scientist bent on world domination. Another variation is the scientist as a naïve, apolitical savant whose discoveries are acquired by power-mad politicians and military officials for nefarious purposes.[39]

CLASS QUESTIONS AND EXERCISES

After reading H. G. Wells's "The Land Ironclads," answer the following questions:

1. How does Wells describe the protagonists in his story (e.g., does he use racial or physical stereotypes)?
2. Wells set the story as a contrast between two types of warfare. Describe them.
3. What role does technology play in deciding the war?

After reading Philip Francis Nowlan's "Armageddon—2419 A.D." and "The Airlords of Han," answer the following questions:

1. How do these stories reflect the American fear of foreign attack?
2. Can you explain the racialist assumptions of the storyline? Where do the stories fit into anti-Asian biases of the interwar years?

After watching *Things to Come*, answer the following questions:

1. In what ways does the film reflect the 1930s obsession with aerial warfare, and what role does new technology play in the next war?
2. Why does the imaginary global war lead to the destruction of civilization?
3. Describe by the various characters' attitudes toward technology. For example, are they all in favor of technological development, or do some of them fear technology?
4. What arguments are made for the exploration of space?

PRIMARY SOURCE ANALYSIS OF A FUTURE-WAR TALE

Hugo Gernsback's place in the history of science fiction is subject to fierce debate.[40] While some accept him as the father of science fiction for creating such pulp magazines as *Amazing Stories*, others regard him as the false dawn of the genre for sacrificing literary quality to focus on technological prognostication. His contributions to the field were so considerable, however, that the annual awards by the Science Fiction Writers of America, the Hugos, are named in his honor.[41]

Gernsback played a significant role in shaping American literary culture as an innovator of the pulp-magazine format, which he used to promote the science fiction genre.[42] While Gernsback did not create the large-magazine format, he used it in new ways. For example, his Electrical Experimenter (established in 1913) consistently integrates images and text for its articles. It was in this magazine that Gernsback began to systematically publish science fiction stories, primarily as a means of promoting new innovations in technology. Indeed, during World War I, Gernsback's articles and stories highlighted

Figure 3.1: July 1918 cover of Hugo Gernsback's large-format magazine the *Electrical Experimenter*. The image is an example of the technical speculation about future weaponry that is characteristic of the future-war genre. *Courtesy of Public Library of Cincinnati and Hamilton County.*

how science and technology might transform warfare, thus establishing a genre we know today as the future-war story.[43]

Gernsback always pushed the connection, both in his fiction and technical articles, between literary imagination and the prediction of technological developments. A good example of this connection is the article "Will the Germans Bombard New York?"[44] The vivid color cover is directly related to the article's content. In addition, the article demonstrates the integration of image with text and makes for an interesting primary source, which the instructor can direct the students to use in several ways (see sample questions in the next section).

Gernsback begins with a discussion of the Germans' bombing of London and Paris, and this can form the basis of a discussion on how, during the age of total war, the distinction between home front and war front is all too

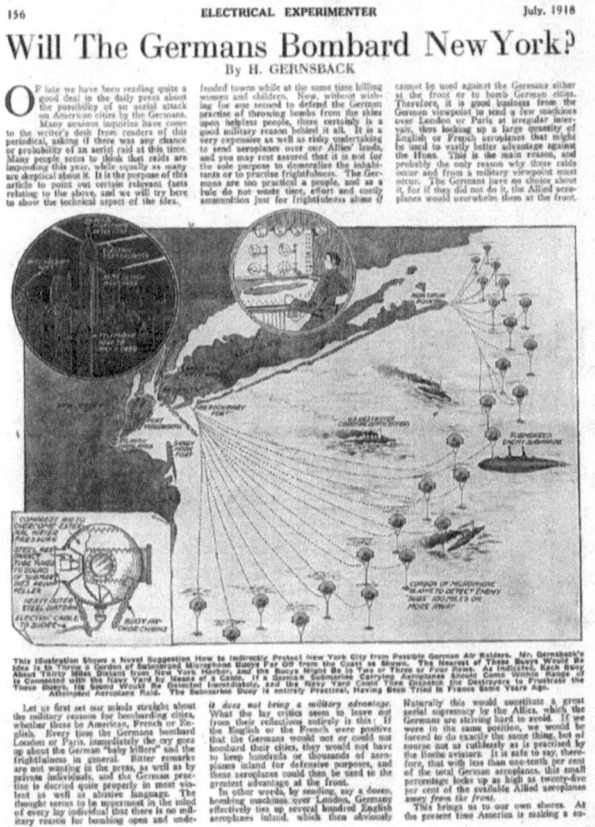

Figure 3.2: First page of Gernsback's article on the technology the Germans could employ to attack New York City during World War I. Note the integration of image and text. *Courtesy of Public Library of Cincinnati and Hamilton County.*

Figure 3.3: Most of the articles and stories in the *Electrical Experimenter* are only a few pages in length. *Courtesy of Public Library of Cincinnati and Hamilton County.*

brief. In analyzing the question of bombing civilians, Gernsback argues that the Germans were "too practical a people, and as a rule do not waste time, effort and costly ammunition just for frightfulness alone *if it does not bring a military advantage.*"[45]

Gernsback hypothesizes that German barbarism toward helpless populations in this new aerial age is the result of careful calculation; forcing the Allies to hold back air assets to protect civilians weakens the front. Thus New York, one of the major embarkation points for troops and supplies to Europe, is a logical target for German attack as a means of disrupting supply lines. It is in the second half of the article that we see perhaps a perfect example of the blending of Gernsback's extrapolation of potential technology to imaginative storytelling. The vulnerability of New York is not to Zeppelins but to submarine-launched airplanes, which he then postulates could easily be developed by the Germans. He rounds out the article with a confident

WILL THE GERMANS BOMBARD NEW YORK?

(Continued from page 157)

tral switchboard as shown in our illustration. The idea of course is to listen in for the whirr of submarine propellers. The Navy Department has a pretty good idea what ships are leaving New York at any time, and in what position these ships should be at any given time. If every outgoing and incoming ship were to take a certain prescribed route, then the work of the listening-in operator would be vastly simplified.

The Navy Department also knows the exact whereabouts of its own submarines, and the propeller sounds of our own ships as well as the sounds of our own submarines, can therefore be eliminated. Then if the operator hears a certain propeller or motor sound which is not located along the regular prescribed routes, he will immediately be informed that the enemy is about and destroyers can be despatched post-haste towards the direction of the buoy from whence the suspicious sounds came.

By means of a subaqueous defense of this kind, it would become an easy matter for the Navy Department to practically make it impossible for the German submarines to break thru the defense unnoticed. In that case it would of course be impossible for the German submarines to assemble their aeroplanes and the attempted raid would be frustrated before it got well under way. A defense of this kind would not be so very costly, and it is certainly practical. Microphone buoys of this kind are usually located from thirty-five feet to fifty feet below the surface, as then the wave motion on top of the ocean will not interfere with the microphones, as at this depth no sound from above reaches them.

On the other hand, these buoys being only small affairs, and being submerged so deeply are quite unseen and unnoticed by the enemy who does not know their whereabouts, this being known only to the Navy Department.

The writer is confident that a device of this kind would help us towards the elimination of the aerial menace, which only fools deny exists.

Figure 3.4: In these large-format magazines, the last 10 percent of a story is often placed at the end of the magazine, probably to get the reader to see the ads. *Courtesy of Public Library of Cincinnati and Hamilton County.*

assertion that the US Navy, using existing and emerging technology, will be able to protect the American homeland from any sustained assault.

CLASS QUESTIONS AND EXERCISES: PRIMARY SOURCE ANALYSIS FOR A FUTURE-WAR TALE

After reading Gernsback's "Will the Germans Bombard New York?" answer the following questions:

1. Do the cover art of the article and the imagery on the first page of the article reflect technological developments, or are they prognostications of potential technology?
2. According to Gernsback, is there any way to protect New York from enemy attack?
3. Does Gernsback deal with the morality of bombing civilians?
4. Does Gernsback believe bombing cities serves a strategic purpose?

NOTES

1. Times [London], "Mr. Baldwin on Aerial Warfare: A Fear for the Future," November 11, 1932, 7.

2. For an analysis of this style of science fiction writing, see the introduction to Frederic Krome, ed., *Fighting the Future War: An Anthology of Science Fiction War Stories, 1914–1945* (New York: Routledge, 2012).

3. Jacques Richardson, "Future War and Superweapons: The Perceptive Fantasies of Albert Robida," *Foresight's* 9, no. 6 (2007): 61–73.

4. H.G. Wells, *Anticipations* (Second Edition; London: Chapman & Hall Ltd, 1902), 197.

5. Wells, *Anticipations*, 285

6. I. F. Clarke, ed., *The Great War with Germany, 1890–1914: Fictions and Fantasies of the War-to-Come* (Liverpool, UK: Liverpool University Press, 1997), 5–6. For an overview of Wells's vision of the future, see W. Warren Wagar, *H. G. Wells: Traversing Time* (Middletown, CT: Wesleyan University Press, 2004).

7. T. H. E. Travers, "H. G. Wells and British Military Theory, 1895–1916," in *War and Society: A Yearbook of Military History*, ed. Brian Bond and Ian Roy, 67–87 (New York: Holms and Meier, 1975).

8. H. G. Wells, "The Land Ironclads," *Strand Magazine* (December 1903), 501–2.

9. H. G. Wells, *The War in the Air*, Bison Frontiers of Imagination (Lincoln: University of Nebraska Press, 2002), 258.

10. David Smith, *H. G. Wells: Desperately Mortal* (New Haven, CT: Yale University Press, 1987), 64.

11. Alfred Gollin, "England Is No Longer an Island: The Phantom Airship Scare of 1909," *Albion* 13, no. 1 (Spring 1981): 43–57.

12. For an analysis of the "Phantom Airship Scare," see Alfred Gollin, *The Impact of Air Power on the British People and Their Government, 1909–14* (Stanford, CA: Stanford University Press, 1989), chap. 3.

13. Frank McConnell, *The Science Fiction of H. G. Wells* (New York: Oxford University Press, 1981), 188.

14. McConnell, *Science Fiction*, 189.

15. On the air war, see Lee B. Kennett, *The First Air War, 1914–1918* (New York: Free Press, 1989); and Denis Winter, *The First of the Few: Fighter Pilots of the First World War* (Athens: University of Georgia Press, 1983).

16. For a sampling of the magazine titles and their covers, see Frank M. Robinson and Lawrence Davidson, *Pulp Culture: The Art of the Fiction Magazine* (Portland, OR: Collectors Press, 2001), 133–45.

17. Besides the future-war story, air-mindedness was pervasive throughout science fiction literature during this era. See Istvan Csicsery-Ronay Jr., "Empire," in *The Routledge Companion to Science Fiction*, ed. Mark Bould, Andrew Butler, Adam Roberts, and Sherryl Vint, 365–66 (New York: Routledge, 2009).

18. Robert Wohl, *A Passion for Wings: Aviation and the Western Imagination, 1908–1918* (New Haven, CT: Yale University Press, 1994), 257. See also Robert Wohl, *The Spectacle of Flight: Aviation and the Western Imagination, 1920–1950* (New Haven, CT: Yale University Press, 2005).

19. For an interesting analysis on the prewar interest in flight, see Peter Demetz, *The Air Show at Brescia, 1909* (New York: Farrar, Straus, and Giroux, 2002).

20. See recent work on the place of air power in modern German history in Guillaume de Syon, *Zeppelin! Germany and the Airship, 1900–1939* (Baltimore, MD: Johns Hopkins University Press, 2002); and Peter Fritz, *A Nation of Flyers: German Aviation and the Popular Imagination* (Cambridge, MA: Harvard University Press, 1992). For the impact of aviation on Russian history, see Scott W. Palmer, *Dictatorship of the Air: Aviation Culture and the Fate of Modern Russia* (New York: Cambridge University Press, 2006).

21. See John Gooch, "Attitudes to War in Late Victorian and Edwardian England," in *War and Society: A Yearbook of Military History*, ed. Brian Bond and Ian Roy, 88–102 (New York: Holmes and Meier, 1975); and Daniel Pick, *War Machine: The Rationalisation of Slaughter in the Modern Age* (New Haven, CT: Yale University Press, 1993).

22. I. F. Clarke, *Voices Prophesying War* (Oxford, UK: Oxford University Press, 1992), 131.

23. Modris Ekstein, *Rites of Spring: The Great War and the Birth of the Modern Age* (New York: Anchor Books, 1989); and Paul Fussell, *The Great War and Modern Memory* (New York: Oxford University Press, 1975). For a critique of the two, see Jay Winter, *Remembering War: The Great War between Memory and History in the Twentieth Century* (New Haven, CT: Yale University Press, 2006), chap. 5.

24. Jay Winter, *Sites of Memory, Sites of Mourning: The Great War in European Cultural History* (New York: Cambridge University Press, 1995), 1–8.

25. Heather Masri, *Science Fiction: Stories and Contexts* (New York: Bedford/St. Martin's, 2008), 1.

26. Clarke, *Voices Prophesying War*, 135–36.

27. Everett F. Bleiler, *Science Fiction: The Gernsback Years* (Kent, OH: Kent State University Press, 1998), 310.

28. Interestingly Nowlan's story appeared the year before Floyd Gibbons, *The Red Napoleon* (New York: J. Cape and H. Smith, 1929), which describes a Mongol-like invasion of the United States. David Esposito argues that Gibbons book was the "all-time best-selling American invasion novel" of the era. See David Esposito, "'Abandon New York—Fall Back to Kansas City!' The Invasion Myth in American Culture," *Utopian Studies* 2, nos. 1–2 (1991): 114.

29. Philip Francis Nowlan, *Armageddon 2419 AD* (New York: Ace Books, 1962).

30. Roger Daniels, *Asian America: Chinese and Japanese in the United States since 1850* (Seattle: University of Washington Press, 1990).

31. Susan Sontag, "The Imagination of Disaster," *Commentary* (October 1965): 42–48.

32. The US edition was published by Macmillan in 1933.

33. See, for example, H. G. Wells's letter to Arthur Bliss on October 17, 1934, in which Wells details the basic narrative of the film and what type of music he wants for each section. David C. Smith, ed., *The Correspondence of H. G. Wells*, vol. 3, *1919–1934* (London: Pickering and Chatto, 1998), letter 2019.

34. For a recent analysis of the film and its place in popular culture, see James Chapman and Nicholas Cull, *Projecting Tomorrow: Science Fiction and Popular Culture* (London: I. B. Taurus, 2013), chap. 2.

35. For the history of the film, see Christopher Frayling, *Things to Come* (London: British Film Institute, 1995). On the fear of aerial assault, see Uri Bialer, *The Shadow of the Bomber: The Fear of Air Attack and British Politics* (London: Royal Historical Society, 1980), 2.

36. The full script for the film, including scenes that never made the final version, can be found at https://leonscripts.tripod.com/scripts/THINGSTOCOME.htm.

37. See Timo Baumann and Daniel Marc Segesser, "Shadows of Total War in French and British Military Journals, 1918–1939," in *The Shadows of Total War: Europe, East Asia, and the United States, 1919–1939*, ed. Roger Chickering and Stig Förster, 197–222 (New York: German Historical Institute and Cambridge University Press, 2003), for how the war was debated by British and French military theorists. See also Bernd Greiner, "'The Study of the Distant Past Is Futile': American Reflections on New Military Frontiers," in *The Shadows of Total War: Europe, East Asia, and the United States, 1919–1939*, ed. Roger Chickering and Stig Förster, 239–51 (New York: German Historical Institute and Cambridge University Press, 2003), for the debates among American military theorists.

38. See the insightful analysis in Clarke, *Voices Prophesying War*, chap. 5.

39. On the changing image of the scientist, see Christopher Frayling, *Mad, Bad and Dangerous? The Scientist and the Cinema* (London: Reaktion Books, 2005). For the interwar period, see especially chapter 4.

40. For biographical details on Hugo Gernsback, see Mike Ashley and Robert A. W. Lowndes, *The Gernsback Days: A Study of the Evolution of Modern Science Fiction from 1911 to 1936* (Holicong, PA: Wildside Press, 2004); Encyclopedia of World Biography Online, "Hugo Gernsback," 2013; James Gleick, "The Making of Future Man," *New York Review of Books*, January 1, 2017.

41. On his death in 1967, the *New York Times* dubbed Hugo Gernsback the "father of science fiction." See the obituary on Hugo Gernsback in Fabian Bachrach, "Hugo Gernsback Is Dead at 83; Author, Publisher and Inventor; 'Father of Modern Science Fiction' Predicted Radar—Beamed TV in '28 'One to Forsee for All,'" *New York Times*, August 20, 1967. For an analysis of Gernsback's significance, see John Cheng, *Astounding Wonder: Imagining Science and Science Fiction in Interwar America* (Philadelphia: University of Pennsylvania Press, 2012), 43–50.

42. See Amanda Hinnant and Berkley Hudson, "The Magazine Revolution, 1880–1920," in *The Oxford History of Popular Print Culture*, vol. 6, *US Popular Print Culture, 1860–1920*, ed. Gary Kelly, 113–31 (New York: Oxford University Press, 2012).

43. The material on Gernsback is take from Frederic Krome, "'Will the Germans Bombard New York?' Hugo Gernsback and the Future War Tale," *Journal of Military History* 86, no. 1 (January 2022): 54–76.

44. Hugo Gernsback, "Will the Germans Bomb New York?" *Electrical Experimenter* 6, no. 3 (July 1918): 156–57, 192, is available in Krome, *Fighting the Future War*, 42–46. For those wanting a digital copy of the original https://archive.org/details/electricalex619181919gern/page/n159/mode/2up.

45. In Krome, *Fighting the Future War*, 42. Emphasis in original.

SUGGESTED READINGS

Bialer, Uri. *The Shadow of the Bomber: The Fear of Air Attack and British Politics*. London: Royal Historical Society, 1980.

Clarke, I. F. *Voices Prophesying War: Future Wars, 1763–3749*. Oxford, UK: Oxford University Press, 1992.

de Syon, Guillaume. *Zeppelin! Germany and the Airship, 1900–1939*. Baltimore, MD: Johns Hopkins University Press, 2002.

Frayling, Christopher. *Mad, Bad and Dangerous? The Scientist and the Cinema*. London: Reaktion Books, 2005.

Fussell, Paul. *The Great War and Modern Memory*. New York: Oxford University Press, 1975.

Krome, Frederic, ed. *Fighting the Future War: An Anthology of Science Fiction War Stories, 1914–1945*. New York: Routledge, 2012.

Overy, Richard. *The Morbid Age: Britain between the Wars*. London: Allen Lane, 2009.

Palmer, Scott W. *Dictatorship of the Air: Aviation Culture and the Fate of Modern Russia*. New York: Cambridge University Press, 2006.

Rottenstiner, Franz, ed. *The Black Mirror and Other Stories: An Anthology of Science Fiction from Germany and Austria*. Translated by Mike Mitchell. Middletown, CT: Wesleyan University Press, 2008.

Winter, Jay. *Sites of Memory, Sites of Mourning: The Great War in European Cultural History*. New York: Cambridge University Press, 1995.

Wohl, Robert. *A Passion for Wings: Aviation and the Western Imagination, 1908–1918*. New Haven, CT: Yale University Press, 1994.

———. *The Spectacle of Flight: Aviation and the Western Imagination, 1920–1950*. New Haven, CT: Yale University Press, 2005.

Chapter 4

Science Fiction and the Holocaust

This chapter provides insight into how science fiction can be used to teach the history and memory of the Holocaust. In particular, it focuses on such issues as how American popular culture has used the Holocaust to teach moral lessons.

Classes this lesson can be used for:

- World history
- US history
- The Holocaust
- Film and the Holocaust
- Introduction to liberal arts
- Introduction to historical methods

Science fiction films and texts:

- *Fatherland*, directed by Christopher Menaul, written by Robert Harris, Stanley Weiser, and Ron Hutchinson (HBO Pictures, 1994)
- Richard Harris, *Fatherland* (New York: Random House, 2006)
- Cyril M. Kornbluth, "Two Dooms," Venture Science Fiction 2, no. 4 (July 1958): 4–49
- Sinclair Lewis, *It Can't Happen Here: A Novel* (Garden City, NY: Doubleday, Doran, 1935)
- Ian R. MacLeod, "The Summer Isles," *Asimov's Science Fiction* 22, nos. 10/11 (October/November 1998): 172–226
- Richard Mueller, "Jew If by Sea," *Fantasy and Science Fiction* (May 2004)
- Nat Schachner, "Ancestral Voices," *Astounding Stories* 12, no. 4 (December 1933): 70–82

- *Twilight Zone*, season 3, episode 9, "Deaths-Head Revisited," directed by Don Medford, written by Rod Serling (aired November 10, 1961, on CBS)
- *Twilight Zone*, season 4, episode 4, "He's Alive," directed by Stuart Rosenberg, written by Rod Serling (aired January 24, 1963, on CBS)

Most history teachers have a familiarity with the literary sources of the Holocaust, such as the *Diary of Anne Frank*, as well as cinematic sources, such as *Schindler's List*. Instructors might, however, be shocked to discover that science fiction authors and filmmakers confronted the dangers of Nazism almost from the moment Hitler came to power. In addition to providing contemporaneous warnings about the dangers of fascism, the Holocaust figures prominently in a variety of science fiction subgenres after 1945. As with other subjects addressed in this volume, the available material offers provocative paths for teaching.

This chapter provides three different approaches to using science fiction for teaching about the Holocaust:

1. Critiques of Nazi racial ideology written in the 1930s that can be used in a US history class.
2. "Americanizing" the Holocaust for discussions about postwar American society and politics.
3. Alternate history and the "it can't happen here" scenario, which can be used in a variety of classes.

CRITIQUES OF NAZI RACIAL IDEOLOGY

For those who choose to examine how science fiction dealt with the rise of Nazism during the 1930s, one of the most fascinating sources for stories are the pulp magazines. The heyday of the pulps—inexpensive large-format magazines printed on cheap pulp paper—was the interwar years. Certainly, many of the stories do not qualify as brilliant literature; however, it is important to remember that what the public reads and what becomes canonical literature are often two separate things.

A prominent figure in the campaign against the rise of authoritarianism was American Jewish author Nat Schachner (1895–1955), whose output of science fiction stories in the pulp magazines during the interwar years was prodigious.[1] One of Schachner's earliest stories critiquing Nazi racial ideology was "Ancestral Voices" (published in the December 1933 issue of *Astounding Stories*). "Ancestral Voices" is a series of vignettes around the central story of an egotistical mad scientist who has invented a time machine. Each vignette juxtaposes racially stereotyped characters: for example, a boxing match between American Jew Max Bernstein and the Nordic champion Hans Schilling, and James Mann, a bookkeeper who, because of his ancestry (one of his progenitors "signed the Domesday book in illiterate, highly illegible Anglo-Saxon"), thought himself superior to his boss, whose Spanish features were "darkly predatory."[2] Schachner also lampoons Herr Hellwig, the dictator of "Mideuropa." As the character is illustrated as a short, dark man with a small mustache, giving a Nazi salute, this is an obvious play on Hitler.

Georgiana Cabot, a daughter of the American Revolution, chides her husband for his "low-bred taste," while in another scene, young Emily learns that her boyfriend Paul's family, descended from a sailor knighted by Queen Elizabeth I, rejects her because her olive-hued skin betrays her Mediterranean ancestry.

The story then cuts to a certain Emmet Pennypacker, the quintessentially mad scientist, who is preparing to visit the past in his time machine. Drunk on his own glory, Pennypacker proclaims that his name will resound through the ages as the "greatest man of all time." He will visit the past because the "future is a myth: they'll accuse me of inventing it." Traveling to the past, meanwhile, will be more difficult, more dangerous, and more readily believed, thereby bringing him greater glory.[3]

The story cuts away briefly to Mr. Murphy, who, in stereotypical Irish fashion, is drunk and accuses his wife of infidelity. After all, the youngest of his three children has the look of an "Eytalian" rather than the traditional Irish features of his other offspring. Meanwhile, in the boxing ring, things are getting personal, as Schilling calls Bernstein a "kike," and Bernstein responds by decking the German. Pennypacker, meanwhile, travels back to the fifth century and witnesses the destruction of a Roman city by a horde of barbarians. In the process of observing the wanton destruction, the time traveler kills a barbarian chieftain who resembles Attila the Hun, an event that turns out to result in Pennypacker's destruction.

Meanwhile, back in 1935, James Mann vanishes mid–xenophobic rant; Herr Hellwig vaporizes mid-anti-Semitic rant; nothing is left of Georgiana Cabot but a dissipating haze; and Emily finds herself alone on the park bench she recently shared with Paul. Amazingly, Bernstein and Schilling both disappear in front of thousands of spectators. Meanwhile, back at the Murphy home, Mr. Murphy comes home drunk to find that his two "golden children" have disappeared. Mrs. Murphy informs her husband that the youngest child was in fact his, while the other two were not.

It seems that when Pennypacker killed the Hun, he killed his own ancestor, thereby destroying his own existence. What's more, the death of the Hun created what Schachner calls a "holocaust" in which 50,000 people in 1935 are vaporized, revealing that a diverse group of different racial types all descend from an Asiatic barbarian. While the moral is clear, that racial assumptions are invalid, the storyline is certainly not coherent—as several subsequent letters to the editor pointed out; such a scenario would wipe out the very existence of people, and no one would ever know they had existed.

Schachner's goal was not only to ridicule those who saw themselves as superior by dint of inheritance but also to challenge the very notion of racial descent; after all, the Jew and the German both vanish because of the mad scientist's actions. Although the story and its author are virtually unknown today outside of a small number of science fiction fans, when it appeared, according to historian Paul Carter, it was in fact the "first shot in pulp science fiction's ragged but earnest crusade against Hitler and fascism."[4]

Schachner often used his pulp science fiction as a mechanism of social and political commentary. Superficially, "Ancestral Voices" seems a mere play on a conventional science fiction trope, yet an examination of the context of Schachner's career reveals a greater nuance to the story. While Schachner made a living as a writer, he also spent much of his adult life combating anti-Semitism in the United States, eventually becoming the legal advisor to the American Jewish Committee, one of the preeminent Jewish civil rights organizations of the day.[5] This particular story must, therefore, be considered not only in the context of the genre of science fiction but also as part of the American Jewish response to anti-Semitism during the interwar years.[6]

Indeed, Schachner was acutely aware of the role of popular literature in promoting negative stereotypes. In an August 1945 column in *The Writer*, a monthly magazine that provided a forum for authors, Schachner wrote a scathing critique of his profession. The column, "Pulp Writers Have a Job to Do," calls on pulp authors to eschew the use of ethnic and racial stereotypes in their stories. Words, Schachner insists, can be "just as lethal as bullets."[7] In addition to chastising writers for their use of ethnic and religious stereotypes, Schachner also provides a seven-point plan to reform literary images. Juxtaposing this column with many of Schachner's own writings from the 1930s where he uses ethnic stereotypes lays the author open to a certain amount of criticism. Yet coming as it did, as World War II in Europe was ending and the horrors of the Holocaust were being revealed to the wider world, the column can also be regarded as a plea to reform the pulp medium from someone who recognized his own culpability.

THE AMERICANIZATION OF THE HOLOCAUST

While few Americans experienced the Holocaust directly, it has nonetheless come to occupy an important place in popular culture, and not just among

American Jews. Films and books about the Holocaust have proliferated at such a rate over the past twenty years—as have museums, exhibits, and books—that some critics refer derisively to a "Holocaust industry" in the United States.[8]

In the case of Hollywood, the image of the Holocaust that graces the screen is often severely criticized as reflecting a distinctly American frame of reference rather than an accurate historical perspective. Certainly, American film has set a pattern for how the Holocaust is remembered in this country. For our purposes, there are several major characteristics of the cinematic Americanization of the Holocaust. While there are some variations in these themes, depending on the specific film and the period in which it was made, several general patterns remain consistent:

1. The film has a "happy" ending.
2. "Justice" is seen to triumph.
3. The victims' suffering is part of a process of being ennobled, or the victims' suffering is for a purpose. Simply put, Jews die for something; American audiences are not usually shown Jews being killed simply because they are Jews.
4. The victims are "universalized." That is to say, even when the characters are distinctly Jewish, they are representative of the suffering of many groups (i.e., the Jew is a victim among many victims).
5. The Nazis appear as sadistic brutes. This is not to imply many Nazis were not sadistic but rather the depiction removes nuance from the historical record.[9]

We can use Spielberg's *Schindler's List* to demonstrate this point. Although Spielberg's film shows the gratuitous killing of Jews, most victims are not central characters, and as such, we feel minimal pain over their deaths. The cinematic Nazis are largely sadistic brutes led by one of the best screen villains of the 1990s Holocaust films, Ralph Fiennes, who played sadistic camp commandant Amon Goeth. Finally, the film has a happy ending.

Indeed, Spielberg managed to find one of the few stories to come out of the Holocaust that has a happy ending for more than a few dozen individuals. In addition, the suffering Jews are mostly depicted as bearing their persecution with dignity, while a limited amount of justice triumphs when the evil Nazi Amon Goeth is shown being executed after the war. So despite its many cinematic qualities, Spielberg's film is an Americanized vision of the Holocaust.[10]

The "Deaths-Head Revisited" episode of Rod Serling's television show Twilight Zone (original series ran 1959–1965) was not the first American program to use the Holocaust as a theme. It was, however, one of the first science fiction programs in prime time to employ the Holocaust as a vehicle to craft what one historian refers to as an "otherworldly morality play."[11]

Serling did not use recurrent characters or situations in his series, and "Deaths-Head Revisited" first aired several months after the trial of Adolph Eichmann, which was televised live in the United States. Like most episodes in the series, it uses supernatural events and situations to explore social and ethical issues of general relevance to American audiences. The show, in effect, implicitly retries Eichmann in the otherworldly court, admittedly in an abstracted and simplified way. Indeed, it can be argued that the drama is more satisfying than reality.

The main character, Gunter Lutze, is a former guard at Dachau Concentration Camp who fled to South America after the war. Feeling nostalgic for his homeland and hoping people "forgot the little excesses" of the Nazi era, Lutze decides to visit his old stomping grounds. Lutze is the essence of a stereotypical Nazi—a "strutting animal," according to Serling's introduction to the episode—who smiles as he remembers the way he abused the inmates. His reminiscence is interrupted by the appearance of Carl Becker, one of the inmates of the camp, who Lutze mistakenly assumes is one of the camp's caretakers. Becker, it turns out, was murdered by Lutze the "night the Americans approached the camp" and is now the ghostly prosecutor putting Lutze on trial for "crimes against humanity." Found guilty by the celestial court, Lutze is sentenced to feel all the physical torments he inflicted on others and is driven insane by the pain.

A powerful episode, "Deaths-Head Revisited" is an example of the Americanization of the Holocaust. Lutze is depicted as a sadist, and the word *Jew* is not used to describe the victims. Indeed, the victims are universalized when Becker asserts, "Ten million human beings were tortured to death in camps like these." Needless to say, the role of anti-Semitism is not part of the story. Television's technical capacity combined with the genre of science fiction liberates a story from traditional constraints, and viewers are provided with the rewarding spectacle of the victims of Nazism getting justice as the depraved tormentor becomes the victim of his own tortures. In a moving epilogue, Serling emphasizes the importance of memory in preventing such atrocities from occurring again.[12]

"IT CAN'T HAPPEN HERE"

Multiple uses for the Holocaust in political discourse have developed, the most common of which is a warning about the dangers of authoritarianism. Such speculation goes back to the early days of the science fiction genre, with Sinclair Lewis's provocative novel *It Can't Happen Here*.[13] Set in the immediate future of the United States—the 1936 election—the story is told from the perspective of an elderly Vermont journalist named Doremus Jessup. The first part of the book details the rise of a populist politician, Buzz Windrip, who uses the popular frustration with the Great Depression to win the presidential election.

Once in power, Windrip and his secretary, Lee Sarason, who is the gray eminence behind the crude politician, consolidate power like fascist Italy and Nazi Germany: curtailing press freedom, using a militia called the Minute Men to intimidate his opponents, and temporarily suspending the constitution. As with other totalitarian regimes, a series of concentration camps is established, and after participating in a clandestine resistance cell, Jessup is sentenced to one, where he is routinely abused by the guards.

Meanwhile, the central government, mismanaged and corrupt, finds itself facing armed uprisings, which the increasingly paranoid Windrip is unable to suppress. While the dictator and his secretary are eventually overthrown in a coup, the new leadership starts a war with Mexico to try to rally the populace. Jessup, now part of a resistance movement in Minnesota, continues to undermine the regime as the war with Mexico has reached a stalemate. While the novel mimics many contemporary events, it was written when none of the totalitarian regimes in Europe had fallen. The triumph of democracy, in other words, is not assured.

Now Lewis's book can be applied to the earlier section of this chapter on contemporaneous responses to the rise of fascism. Yet Lewis's work is one of the prototexts of the alternate-history subgenre, which remains a popular concept in science fiction. For example, in addition to the Nazis winning World War II, some popular themes of alternate history are the failure of the American Revolution and the South winning the Civil War. The key to the subgenre is that, at some crucial point in history, a divergence occurs. For example, in Robert Harris's alternate-history novel *Fatherland*, the failure of the D-Day invasion leads the United States to withdraw from the war and the Nazi regime to survive.[14]

Historian Gavriel Rosenfeld argues that the scenario of the Nazis winning the war or the United States not entering it usually serves a political purpose. As with most science fiction stories, a form of "presentist exploration" of the past serves as a mechanism to comment on contemporary events in which describing how the past might have been different reflects either hope or fear.[15]

Rosenfeld places these stories into two primary categories: the nightmare scenario and the fantasy scenario. In the fantasy scenario, the alternate variation of the past is superior to the actual history. The goal of such stories is to express dissatisfaction with the present. Such writing tends, according to Rosenfeld, to be prominent among liberals, as the present is seen as wanting.

In the nightmare scenario, the present reality is okay and does not need to be changed. Such writings, Rosenfeld believes, tend toward conservative political ideology. Rosenfeld concedes that fantasy scenarios, like the South winning the Civil War, can be used for a conservative vision of the present, while liberals can certainly use a nightmare to express dissatisfaction with how history turned out. For such political musings, the idea of a Nazi victory, combined perhaps with the rise of a totalitarian state in the United States or Great Britain, can be used for some very intense classroom discussions.[16]

Robert Harris's *Fatherland* can also provide a fruitful set of class projects, for it was also adapted into a film.[17] Both novel and film can be used by instructors, either independently or in conjunction, although as the latter is closer to being an example of the Americanization of the Holocaust than the original story.

The novel is set in 1964 Berlin, and Adolph Hitler is about to celebrate his seventy-fifth birthday with a new détente with the United States. The story revolves around two characters, Xavier March, a Berlin detective investigating a series of murders of old-guard Nazi officials, and Charlotte "Charlie" Maguire, an American journalist who by chance is thrown together with March as they uncover the conspiracy behind the murders. All of those killed were active in implementing the Holocaust, and the reason behind the secret purge is to cover up the crimes so the Nazi regime can turn the Cold War with the United States into a more formal alliance. As March and Maguire discover the secrets of the Holocaust, March realizes that he and the rest of German society always knew the truth but refused to admit it.

In a confrontation with a colleague, who, like so many others (in real life and in this alternate history), claims, "I didn't know," March retorts, "Of course you knew! Every time someone made a joke about 'going East,' every time you heard a mother tell her children to behave or they'd go up the chimney. We knew when we moved into their houses, when we took their property, their jobs. We knew but we didn't have the facts."[18] The novel ends with Maguire smuggling crucial historical documents across the border into Switzerland, while March travels to Auschwitz to make a final diversionary stand and die in a shootout, perhaps to symbolically atone for the sins of his people.

The American-made movie version of *Fatherland* diverges from the novel in some important ways and is instructive in how the Holocaust continues to be Americanized, even into the 1990s. The two main characters—March and Maguire—are the same, and the dark conspiracy is also the same. In the film, however, March maintains that he did not know about the Holocaust. "I was at sea," he tells Charlie of his time as a wartime submariner, and when he returned home, he had no reason to doubt the official story that story of the Jews being "resettled in the East." Maguire takes the incriminating documents to the visiting American president, Joseph Kennedy Sr., who upon seeing them calls off the impending alliance with Nazi Germany. March is killed in a shootout, and Maguire is arrested and presumably executed by the Nazis.

How, then, is the cinematic story Americanized? In both novel and film, the Nazis' victims are clearly labeled as Jewish. Yet many of the Nazis fit the prevailing stereotype of brutish thugs. While both March and Maguire, the heroes of the story, die, justice can be said to triumph, as the failure of the American alliance will eventually lead to the downfall of the Nazi regime. This is revealed by the film's narrator, who turns out to be Xavier March's son and who at the end proclaims his pride in his father's role in destroying the evil empire.

It is interesting that the themes of "it can't happen here" and the Axis winning World War II are in fact closely linked in the genre. The potential for a nightmare scenario, in which not only do the Nazis win but America and Britain also become bastions of authoritarianism, are used multiple times over the decades after 1945. While some books and television programs, such as Philip K. Dick's *The Man in the High Castle* and its TV adaptation, are well known and can certainly be used in the classroom, I again suggest some lesser-known texts for possible classroom use.[19]

One such example that instructors can use is Ian R. MacLeod's "The Summer Isles."[20] MacLeod's novella superficially might seem to have little to do with the Holocaust. In this deviation from actual history, the Germans won World War I, and in the aftermath of this humiliating defeat, Britain's history followed a version of Weimar Germany, in which a weak democratic government gave way to a totalitarian regime. Like Nazi Germany, the British fascist state is a corrupt militaristic state that sends Jews and "sexual deviants" to the "summer isles" (i.e., concentration/death camps), from which none return.

The story is told from the perspective of an aging Oxford don, whose secret is not only that he is gay but also that, as a young man, he had an affair with John Arthur, the charismatic leader of the state. Frustrated by his hidden life and knowing that he has little time left to live, the narrator decides to assassinate Arthur in the hopes of restoring British democracy. Although he fails in his plot, the dictator is overthrown in a bloody coup, but like Lewis's story, democracy is not restored to Britain. Although not explicitly about the Holocaust, MacLeod sets up an alternate-history scenario that, like Sinclair Lewis's, challenges the reader and our perhaps comfortable assumption that democracy in the Anglophone world will always triumph over authoritarianism.

When studying the Holocaust, it quickly becomes apparent that almost every aspect can be discussed as an ethical challenge. "What would you do if" is, of course, among the most common questions, especially if it relates to placing yourself in the position of the victim, perpetrator, or bystander. A relatively unknown alternate-history story from 2004 by Richard Mueller, "Jew If by Sea," provides some fascinating avenues for the instructor to consider ethical questions.[21] In this story, the point of historical divergence occurs when a cease-fire is declared (perhaps 1943 or 1944), leaving the Nazis dominant on the Continent. While President Dewey (FDR, apparently having lost the 1944 election) promises to continue to uphold the alliance with Britain, most Americans are war weary. Much of the British Empire, such as India, has declared independence, and Vichy France maintains control over several overseas colonies.

The story takes place some eight months after the cease-fire, characterized as an "undeclared peace and a dormant war" by the narrator, who is an officer commanding an American submarine patrolling the Indian Ocean. In this timeline, the Germans have implemented the "Madagascar Plan," an idea first floated in 1940 to resettle Europe's Jews on the island. Place in temporary command of the US submarine, and with a Free French intelligence officer as liaison, the narrator is ordered to find a German "repatriation" vessel supposedly transporting Jews to Madagascar. Although many Americans prefer to believe the Nazi statements that they are resettling Europe's Jews, "Warhawk Democrats" in the United States dispute this story, and US military intelligence wants to get to the truth. The patrol will take the sub perilously close to a Nazi no-go zone, and the American officer is given verbal command to "exceed" his orders as he sees fit.

On the way to the Nazi exclusion zone, the sub rescues a man who turns out to have been a Jew on one of the transports. He tells a frightening tale of transportees being told they were being shipped to Madagascar, but in the middle of the Indian Ocean, the center of their ship opened, using an ingenious series of gears and levers, and all the passengers were dumped into shark-infested waters. He is the only survivor. Upon finding the German repatriation vessel, determining the truth of the survivor's account, and knowing it will likely rekindle the war, the American officer orders the destruction of the Nazi ship and the rescuing of as many passengers as possible.

As a stand-alone story, Mueller's tale is an interesting example to which we can apply Rosenfeld's typologies, and indeed, when discussed in a classroom setting, students often divide just about evenly between saying it is a nightmare or fantasy scenario. In the context of contemporary politics, it was published when not only was memory of the Holocaust fading but also the United States was engaged in a vigorous debate about its role in the world. A willingness to continue fighting the war to save Europe's Jews was never a stated goal of the grand alliance. In addition, an underlying theme of the story is whether it was worth war to save a persecuted people, which in the early twenty-first century was one of the arguments for war in Afghanistan and Iraq.

CLASS QUESTIONS AND EXERCISES: CRITIQUES OF NAZI RACIAL IDEOLOGY

1. Do a bibliographic search of Nat Schachner stories. Can you determine from a sample of his writings on contemporary political issues where his politics fit into 1930s America? For example, would you call his views conservative or liberal?
2. Read "Ancestral Voices" and "Pulp Writers Have a Job to Do." How does Schachner use ethnic stereotypes in history? Does the story provide an effective critique of racial bigotry? What does Schachner say his fellow writers can do to help end bigotry?

CLASS QUESTIONS AND EXERCISES: THE AMERICANIZATION OF THE HOLOCAUST

1. Identify the basic characteristics of the Americanization of the Holocaust from 1945 to 1975.
2. After describing the basic characteristics of the Americanization of the Holocaust in film and television, watch the *Twilight Zone* episode "Deaths-Head Revisited." How would you analyze this television program as an example of the Americanization of the Holocaust? Use specific examples in your answer.

CLASS QUESTIONS AND EXERCISES: "IT CAN'T HAPPEN HERE"

1. Read Gavriel Rosenfeld, "Why Do We Ask 'What If?'" and then Cyril M. Kornbluth's "Two Dooms," Ian R. MacLeod's "The Summer Isles," and Richard Mueller's "Jew If by Sea." Explain the two major allohistorical scenarios Rosenfeld identifies and what political purposes they usually serve. Summarize the basic premise of the Kornbluth, MacLeod, and Mueller stories. Do they fit into Rosenfeld's political typologies? If so, explain how. Do any of these stories tell us about how the Nazi era is used in popular culture to make political statements?

NOTES

1. John Clute and Peter Nicholas, *The Encyclopedia of Science Fiction*, 3rd ed. (London: Orbit, 1999), 1056. Isaac Asimov credited Schachner as a major influence

on his decision to become a writer. Asimov's comments on Schachner are in Isaac Asimov, ed., *Before the Golden Age: A Science Fiction Anthology of the 1930s* (Garden City, NY: Doubleday, 1974), 842.

2. Nat Schachner, "Ancestral Voices," *Astounding Stories* 12, no. 4 (December 1933): 71.

3. Schachner, "Ancestral Voices," 73–74.

4. Paul A. Carter, "From 'Nat' to 'Nathan': The Liberal Arts Odyssey of a Pulpster," in *Styles of Creation: Aesthetic Techniques and the Creation of Fictional Worlds*, ed. George Slusser and Eric S. Rabkin, 58–78 (Athens: University of Georgia Press, 1992), 59.

5. See Nat Schachner, *The Price of Liberty: A History of the American Jewish Committee* (New York: American Jewish Committee, 1948).

6. For this interpretation, see Henry Feingold, *Zion in America: The Jewish Experience from Colonial Times to the Present* (Mineola, NY: Dover, 2002), 142.

7. Nathan Schachner, "Pulp Writers Have a Job to Do," *The Writer* (August 1945), 244.

8. For a sample of the debate, see Peter Novick, *The Holocaust in American Life* (Boston: Houghton Mifflin, 1999).

9. For various discussions about this issue, see Hilene Flanzbaum, ed., *The Americanization of the Holocaust* (Baltimore, MD: Johns Hopkins University Press, 1999).

10. See Stephen J. Whitfield, "Shoah," in *In Search of American Jewish Culture* (Hanover, NH: University Press of New England, 1999), for an analysis of the place of *Schindler's List* in the cultural landscape.

11. Joel Engel, *Rod Serling: The Dreams and Nightmares of Life in the Twilight Zone: A Biography* (Chicago: Contemporary Books, 1989) 189.

12. For an analysis of this particular episode and ideas for other shows to use in class, see Jeffrey Shandler, "Aliens in the Wasteland: American Encounters with the Holocaust on 1960s Science Fiction Television," in *The Americanization of the Holocaust*, ed. Hilene Flanzbaum, 33–44 (Baltimore, MD: Johns Hopkins University Press, 1999).

13. Sinclair Lewis, *It Can't Happen Here: A Novel* (Garden City, NY: Doubleday, Doran, 1935).

14. Robert Harris, *Fatherland* (New York: Random House, 2006).

15. Rosenfeld first proposed these ideas in Gavriel D. Rosenfeld, "Why Do We Ask 'What If?' Reflections on the Function of Alternate History," *History and Theory*, theme issue 41 (December 2002): 90–103. Later he expanded it in Gavriel D. Rosenfeld, *The World Hitler Never Made: Alternate History and the Memory of Nazism* (New York: Cambridge University Press, 2005).

16. Rosenfeld, *World Hitler Never Made*, 10–11.

17. *Fatherland*, dir. Christopher Menaul, writ. Robert Harris, Stanley Weiser, and Ron Hutchinson (HBO Pictures, 1994).

18. Harris, *Fatherland*, 311.

19. Philip K. Dick, *The Man in the High Castle: A Novel* (New York: Putnam, 1962); *Man in the High Castle*, created by Frank Spotnitz, aired 2015–2019 on Amazon Prime Video.

20. Ian R. MacLeod, "The Summer Isles," originally published in *Asimov's Science Fiction Magazine* 22, nos. 10/11 (October/November 1988): 172–226. It was later expanded into a book.

21. Richard Mueller, "Jew If by Sea," *Fantasy and Science Fiction Magazine* (May 2004).

SUGGESTED READING

Carter, Paul A. "The Phantom Dictator: Science Fiction Discovers Hitler." In *The Creation of Tomorrow: Fifty Years of Magazine Science Fiction*. New York: Columbia University Press, 1977.

Krantz, Charles. "Teaching *Night and Fog*: History and Historiography." *Film and History: An Interdisciplinary Journal of Film and Television Studies* 15, no. 1 (February 1985): 1–11.

Langer, Lawrence. "The Americanization of the Holocaust on Stage and Screen." In *Admitting the Holocaust: Collected Essays*. New York: Oxford University Press, 1995.

Rosenfeld, Gavriel D. "Why Do We Ask 'What If?' Reflections on the Function of Alternate History." *History and Theory*, theme issue 41 (December 2002): 90–103.

———. *The World Hitler Never Made: Alternate History and the Memory of Nazism*. New York: Cambridge University Press, 2005.

Schachner, Nat. "Pulp Authors Have a Job to Do." *Writer* (August 1945).

Shandler, Jeffrey. "Aliens in the Wasteland: American Encounters with the Holocaust on 1960s Science Fiction Television." In *The Americanization of the Holocaust*, edited by Hilene Flanzbaum, 33–44 Baltimore, MD: Johns Hopkins University Press, 1999.

———. *While America Watches: Televising the Holocaust*. New York: Oxford University Press, 2000.

Chapter 5

Mutations and Monsters

Cold War Anxiety in the 1950s and '60s

This chapter provides several examples of Cold War–era films and text from the Anglophone world. Each represents an expression of the anxieties brought on by the nuclear age.

Classes this lesson can be used for:

- Modern world history
- Cold War/popular culture of the Cold War
- US history since 1945
- Introduction to historical methodology

Science fiction films and texts:

- *Them!*, directed by Gordon Douglas, written by Ted Sherdeman, Russell S. Hughes, and George Worthing Yates (Warner Bros., 1954)
- *Twilight Zone*, season 1, episode 22, "The Monsters Are Due on Maple Street," directed by Ron Winston, written by Rod Serling (aired March 4, 1960, on CBS)
- John Wyndham, *The Chrysalids* (1955; New York: New York Review Books, 2008)

Looking for science fiction sources to teach the popular culture of the Cold War era can easily overwhelm the instructor. Indeed, the sheer volume of material produced during the Cold War is matched only by the variety of subjects, ranging from alien invasions to postapocalyptic worlds.[1] For example, consider how alien-invasion stories can fit into Cold War pedagogy; the original *The Body Snatchers*, describes a covert assault by alien pods with a singular goal (replacing humans with alien doubles) and singular consciousness (no emotions, emotional attachments, or conflicts).[2] The pod invaders can be viewed as either a surrogate for the Communist threat or a metaphor for the paranoia of McCarthyism and its demands for intellectual conformity. Both subjects fit easily within the course outcomes of a variety of classes.[3]

Although trying to determine which sources to use in the classroom within the broader theme of science fiction and the Cold War is potentially intimidating, it can also be an opportunity. Simply put, the volume of material enables the instructor to be flexible with choice of films or texts, and instructors can also use transnational sources, thereby adapting the material to US, European, or world history.[4]

This chapter focuses on the film *Them!*, British novelist John Wyndham's *The Chrysalids*, and the *Twilight Zone* episode "The Monsters Are Due on Maple Street."[5] Moreover, each represents an example of the anxieties that were a product of the nuclear age and the Cold War. Each is not only an excellent source about dealing with the anxieties of the early nuclear age (1945–1965), but they also raise questions about such issues as the control of information, religious extremism, and how easily the social bonds that tie communities together can be undone.

NUCLEAR ANXIETY: *THEM!*

Carl Abbott argues that, where pre-1945 science fiction stories often looked to technology to fix the world, in the aftermath of the mass aerial bombardment of cities and the atomic bombings of Hiroshima and Nagasaki, writers were more likely to wonder if that technology would destroy humanity rather than save it.[6] The development of nuclear anxiety in the post-1945 era cuts across national boundaries. It is useful, therefore, for the instructor to set the context for these texts by first discussing the social impact of the World War II strategic-bombing campaign and then the development of the Cold War so students understand the rise of anxiety about the nuclear age.

This sets the stage for students to watch the 1954 film *Them!*, which was the highest-grossing Hollywood film of that year. The film begins in the New Mexico desert, where state trooper Ben Peterson and his partner find a little girl wandering alone and unable to speak due to shock. While investigating, the troopers find that the child's family is missing under strange circumstances. Over the next few days, more people disappear, including Peterson's partner. FBI agent Robert Graham joins the case and is baffled because none of the clues to the disappearances add up.

One particularly baffling piece of evidence is what appears to be a strange footprint that no local expert can identify. No one, that is, until a father-daughter team—the Medfords, who work for the US Department of Agriculture—arrives to solve the riddle.[7] The Medfords are insect specialists and deduce from the evidence that humanity is facing a grave danger, so grave that, if knowledge of it is released, it could lead to a "nationwide panic"—for the disappearances are due to the appearance of a mutant colony of giant ants created by lingering fallout from the first atomic bomb tests in New Mexico in 1945. It seems these mutant ants have started to feed on the human population.[8]

Using the Medfords' expertise, the ant colony is located and destroyed but not before two queen ants escape. The scene then shifts to Washington, DC, where the elder Dr. Medford gives a tutorial on ant etymology to political and military officials. Once again, the issue of keeping the information from the public is raised. New Mexico State Trooper Peterson argues that, for the public good, absolute secrecy must be maintained. "I don't know of a police department in the world," he tells the officials, "that could handle the panic if the public knew these babies were loose."

The briefing ends with the senior Medford saying that, unless the missing queen ants are destroyed before they can hatch more queens, humanity will be extinct within a year. Fortunately, one of the queen ants is located aboard a large cargo vessel at sea, and while the unfortunate crew cannot be saved, the emerging ant colony is destroyed. The action then moves to Los Angeles, where the remaining queen ant is discovered to have established a nest in the city sewer system.

Attacking the nest is complicated by the fact that two missing children first need to be rescued, which Peterson accomplishes at the cost of his own life. Once the children are safe, FBI agent Graham leads the military into the sewer and destroys the last giant ant nest before any new queens have escaped. As the film ends with the last ants' burning, Graham wonders if any other creatures will result from subsequent atomic bomb tests. Dr. Medford replies that it is impossible to know: "When man entered the atomic age, he opened the door to a new world. What we may eventually find in that new world, nobody can predict."

One virtue of using this film in class is that the storyline initially appears plausible, although, as in most cases, the specific science is not accurate. The technology used in the film, for example, is the standard police and military hardware available at the time, adding to the credibility of the story. One interesting question that can be addressed, in addition to the issue of nuclear anxiety, is the need for government secrecy.

In classroom discussions about the film and US culture in the 1950s, an interesting exercise was first proposed by a student of mine. If *Them!* was remade today, how would the storyline differ? On a basic level, most students agreed that, rather than the mutation being the inadvertent result of lingering radiation, the giant ants would have been the result of a secret government experiment that got out of hand. The discussion of a science fiction film from the 1950s thus became a wider discussion about attitudes toward the state that have evolved in the last seventy years—an enjoyable intellectual exercise generated by members of the class and not the instructor.

FEAR OF DEVIATIONS IN A POSTAPOCALYPTIC WORLD

John Wyndham's science fiction novel *The Chrysalids* is primarily remembered as an example of the postapocalyptic/post–nuclear war genre that became popular in Britain after 1945.[9] Wyndham (1903–1969) is often associated with a British science fiction genre that author/critic Brian Aldiss calls "the cozy catastrophe."[10] Though Aldiss implies that these stories lack a certain grand narrative, Wyndham is part of a long tradition in apocalyptic literature, going back at least to H. G. Wells, in which catastrophic events are told from a first-person perspective.[11] David Seed argues that Wyndham "embedded his science fiction in the circumstantial detail of daily life" and that Wyndham's "understated method" was used to avoid space-opera melodrama.[12]

In *The Chrysalids*, Wyndham uses religious bigotry and fear of genetic mutation in a postapocalyptic society to establish his major plotline. This society resembles Puritan England/New England, in that government policy is designed to ensure religious virtue. The use of a future theocracy of suppressed individuality is designed to express anxiety about the nuclear age and potential impact of weapons of mass destruction.

Religious zealotry can also be understood to represent fears about unrestrained government power, along with post-1945 British anxieties of sociopolitical decline in the wake of two world wars. For British writers, the duration and cost of these conflagrations, both in human and material terms, often led to pessimism about the potential for a more peaceful society.[13] Thus it will be helpful for the students if the instructor spends some time discussing the experience of Britain's decline as a world power in the twentieth century.

The Chrysalids is told from the perspective of teenager David Strorm, who lives in Waknuk, Labrador, a farming community that is now temperate in climate some two thousand years after "God sent the tribulation"[14] (i.e., nuclear war). Of all the books produced in the "Old World," only the Bible remains. Knowledge of the "tribulations" that destroyed that world is provided in a religious book called *Repentances*, which survived because it was sealed in a stone coffer. Because the communities of Labrador and nearby Newfoundland (Newf) have no knowledge of nuclear war or the lingering effects of radiation, deviations (mutations) are understood as God's punishment for personal or communal sins.

Each community has a local bureaucrat, known as "the Inspector," whose primary function is to certify plants, animals, and people as being in the "true image." When deviations, like deformed or mutated animals, are found they are ceremonially killed in public displays of repentance; for example, with damaged crops, the fields are burned as an offense to the "true image" while hymns are sung. All children must pass an examination by the Inspector and receive a certificate to live in the community.

In ages past, those children who failed to conform to the "true image" were euthanized if their deviation was recognizable at birth or sterilized and exiled to the "fringes" if it developed later in life. The wild and virtually unlivable fringes occupy the space between Labrador's fertile lands and the deadly and radioactive badlands. In the story, newborns are now expelled to the edge of the fringes instead of euthanized; they are often rescued and raised by deviants from the fringes.

David was told his grandfather Elias was a man characterized by his "evangelical fire." He left the coastal settlements and moved inland to escape the "ungodly ways of the East,"[15] although David suspects he was forced to leave due to his extreme religious views. Waknuk was, therefore, initially established as a haven for those who wanted a truly godly community and not the liberalizing larger urban centers. Wyndham adroitly uses historical concepts to tell the story of David's family and the Waknuk community, paralleling the early-seventeenth-century Puritan migration to New England.

Wyndham's postapocalyptic community resembles the *popular* image of Puritan England, with hunts for deviation in lieu of hunts for witches, daily prayers and sermons about sin, and general religious zealotry forming the basis of civil government.[16] David's home is adorned with signs on the walls linking physical difference with sin:

- "Only the Image of God Is Man"
- "Keep Pure the Stock of the Lord"
- "Blessed Is the Norm"
- "Watch Thou for the Mutant"
- "The Devil Is the Father of Deviation"

David grows up in a society where physical differences are a sign of sinfulness; early in the story, David describes his community as being so "God-fearing" that even his being left-handed evoked "slight disapproval."[17] David's father, Joseph, is a regional magistrate and, even by the standards of his community, is regarded as a zealot. One of the root causes of Joseph's religious intensity is revealed later in the novel: David has an uncle who is a deviant exiled to the fringes.

Early in the story, David's faith is shaken when he discovers that one of his friends, a young girl named Sophie, is a deviant. When the authorities discover Sophie's deformity—an extra toe—she is sterilized and exiled to the fringes. This forces David to come to grips with his own difference, for David's secret deviation is that he is a telepath.

Throughout the novel, David strives to understand himself and his place in a world that seeks to maintain a fixed reality. From his Uncle Axel, David develops an understanding of the bigotry and intolerance of his world. Axel was a sailor before he was crippled in an accident; Axel has seen the cosmopolitan world outside Labrador and long since lost his fear of difference. Axel even utters what is perhaps the greatest heresy, challenging the very notion of religious orthodoxy: "I'm telling you that nobody, nobody, really knows what is the true image. They all think they know—just as we think we know, but for all we can prove, the Old People themselves may not have been the true image."[18] When Axel learns that David is one of nine teenagers who can communicate with a pictogram form of telepathy, he cautions the boy to stay silent, lest the religious authorities brand them deviations.

Because most of the telepaths share a common ancestor—David and Rosalind are first cousins—the reader initially assumes that this is a genetic mutation specific to one bloodline. The group maintains its secret existence, at times precariously, until David's younger sister Petra reveals a level of telepathic power that cannot be restrained. Her talent exposes the group to the local religious authorities, and her ability is so powerful that she is even able to communicate with telepaths on the other side of the world in New Zealand. The revelation that an entire race with even greater telepathic power lives in New Zealand (Sealanders) forces the reader to consider that David and his companions may not be mutants; instead, they may represent the next stage of human evolution.

Despite the conservatives' desires to maintain a fixed society, David lives in a world that is showing signs of change. The reader learns from various snippets in the story that the fringes are being cleared, and their despised inhabitants are living a constrained existence, essentially starving. The clearing of additional territory is forcing the inhabitants of Waknuk to confront the detritus of their enforcement of physical conformity.

Even the religious intensity of the region is being transformed. In addition to deviant children being spared—although sterilized and exiled to an impoverished life in the fringes—the brutality of everyday life seems to be diminishing. Waknuk's level of deviance is going down, not necessarily because of decreased mutations, but because people are more liberal in their interpretation of what is the true image, even being willing to eat pigs that are not certified. One old resident even complains about the laxity of standards: "When my father was a young man a woman who bore a child that wasn't in the image was whipped for it. If she bore three out of the image, she was uncertified, outlawed, and sold . . . My father reckoned there was a lot less trouble with mutants on account of it, and when there were any, they were burnt, like other deviations."[19]

People in the district believe that the level of deviation would be lower still but for Joseph, who does not call the Inspector to decide whether plants or animals should be destroyed, preferring to eliminate sin immediately. In several cases, Joseph's religious bigotry comes into conflict with the district Inspector's sense of his job as a bureaucratic process. In one incident, a neighbor is found to have a tailless cat. As a local magistrate, Joseph declares the cat a deviation, orders it destroyed, and is so annoyed when the owners appeal that he dispatches the unfortunate animal himself. When it is revealed that there is indeed a recognized species of cat without a tail, the elder Strorm is forced to issue a public apology and pay restitution.

In a related incident, Joseph's neighbor (and brother-in-law) obtains two oversized horses. The appearance of obvious offenses, according to Joseph, requires immediate action. When he orders the Inspector to issue a warrant for the horses to be put down, the Inspector refuses: "'You're out of order this time,' the Inspector told him cheerfully, glad for once that his position was incontestable. 'They're government-approved, so they are beyond my jurisdiction anyway.'"[20] After Joseph asserts that it is a "moral duty to issue an order against these so-called horses," the Inspector counters that it is "part of my official duty to protect them from harm by fools and bigots."[21]

In the heated exchange between David's father and the Inspector, the reader sees a microcosm of the tensions in postapocalyptic Labrador society. On the one side, Joseph Strorm represents the desire for a static society with fixed norms. He is a man constantly searching for sin, which is manifested in everything from disfigured crops to oversized horses. The Inspector, meanwhile, is not a multicultural liberal; rather he represents the bureaucratic desire for order and rationality. While his definition of *deviation* is more flexible, it does not include acceptance of physical or mental mutations.

When the Inspector and his government discover something amiss with David and his cohort, he is as dogged in his pursuit of sin as any Puritan preacher. Such maniacal pursuit of deviance forms the cornerstone of sociologist Kai Erikson's classic work on nonconformity in Puritan society. Simply put, in order to maintain conformity and therefore manage socioeconomic relationships, a Puritan needed to have deviance in order to define what was normal, and as such, when it was discovered, it had to be contained and explained.[22] As long as David is merely a boy who has a different outlook than his father, the Inspector lacks any real interest in him; when he is revealed to be a "deviant," however, the Inspector (and the government) need to classify him.

The tension between maintaining a fixed society and change explodes when the discovery of the telepaths shakes the religious foundations of Waknuk, for it is a deviance that cannot be detected through normal physical inspection. The level of the authorities' fear is revealed when David, Rosalind, and Petra flee; a massive manhunt follows them all the way to fringes. Though puritanical zeal may be loosening, it still drives the storyline and the roles and relationships of the characters within.

The novel concludes with the New Zealanders rescuing David and his companions and, in the process, killing all their pursuers. This ambiguous ending is one of the key points in using the novel in the classroom. If the New Zealanders represent the next stage of human evolution and can casually kill all those who are different from them, then how do they differ from the religious zealots of David's community? *The Chrysalids* is, therefore, a great example of the historical-ethical discussions that develop in a post-Holocaust world.

MAPLE STREET = EVERY STREET, USA?

A popular conception of American society in the 1950s and early 1960s was that it was largely dominated by communal consensus and intellectual conformity. Over the last few decades, historians have largely challenged those assumptions, and as with many other eras, science fiction is an example of a literature—and, by extension, film and television—of dissent from dominant ideologies.[23]

During its five-season run, Rod Serling's *Twilight Zone* (1959–1964) earned a reputation for challenging the stereotypes and existing norms of American society. "The Monsters Are Due on Maple Street" is one of the most discussed episodes of the series.[24] Set on an eponymous location in the United States (Maple Street could be an example from any town), the episode begins as a summer afternoon wanes and the residents enjoy the usual activities of suburban life: buying ice cream, sitting on the porch, fiddling with cars, and doing home repairs. The residents all know each other on a first-name basis, creating a scene reminiscent of the common TV shows of the era. This is the last moment of sanity for the population.

Normal activities are interrupted by a flash of light and an eerie sound, followed by a complete power outage. Not only are the lights out, but also phones no longer connect, cars do not start, and the residents can't even get static on their portable radios. One neighbor goes over to the next street to discover how widespread the blackout is, and while he is gone, the social fabric of Maple Street society begins to unravel.

When two adults decide to walk into town, a young boy urges them not to go. The young boy represents the baby boomer who consumes the popular culture of his day, in particular the alien-invasion stories beloved of comic books and pulp literature. According to the boy, the invasion starts with an advance team that "looks just like us" and that infiltrates a target before the main invasion occurs.

At first, the boy's suggestion is laughed at, but then, one resident's car starts seemingly by itself. The rest of the residents then start to interrogate the car's owner: Why didn't he rush out to the street when the power went off like everyone else? Why does he walk outside his house late at night looking at the stars? Is he waiting for something? Despite his efforts to defend himself against charges of deviating from the norm, the rest of the block looks at him as being somehow alien. The people on Maple Street have discovered someone is "different," and the cohesiveness of a suburban American community begins to unravel.

As night falls, the situation continues to deteriorate. Some denizens of what was once a peaceful street watch their former friend, now a suspected alien. Steve, one resident, tries to reassert a degree of rationality, and the neighbors' suspicions quickly turn on him. It seems Steve is building a ham radio in his basement. A few hours earlier, such a statement would have elicited nothing more than a few interested queries by the neighbors. Now, it is treated as an accusation, for even a ham radio, one symbol of post-1945 American ingenuity, could be part of an alien plot.

A floodgate has opened, as all hobbies or personal quirks are laid bare, and arguments ensue. Steve once again tries to issue a warning that paranoia will make the neighbors "eat each other up alive." Such rationality is Serling's way of reminding his viewers that the more reasoned responses to McCarthy's Red Scare led to further accusations of Communist infiltration. In the midst of the social disintegration, a shadowy figure is seen walking down the street. In a panic, one resident shoots. The neighbor who earlier in the episode walked to the next street is the first fatality.

Suddenly, lights and engines randomly turn on and off across Maple Street, and the formerly peaceful inhabitants begin to riot and destroy each other's property. As the mayhem continues, the scene pans back to a hilltop and a flying saucer with two humanoid looking aliens working a control board. It turns out that the young boy was partially correct; there was an alien presence, and they were manipulating the power. It seems this is a kind of training exercise:

> FIRST ALIEN: Understand the procedure now? Just stop a few of their machines and radios and telephones and lawn mowers . . . throw them into darkness for a few hours, and then you just sit back and watch the pattern.

SECOND ALIEN: And this pattern is always the same?

FIRST ALIEN: With few variations. They pick the most dangerous enemy they can find . . . and it's themselves. And all we need do is sit back . . . and watch.

SECOND ALIEN: Then I take it this place . . . this Maple Street . . . is not unique.

FIRST ALIEN: By no means. Their world is full of Maple Streets. And we'll go from one to the other and let them destroy themselves. One to the other . . . one to the other . . . one to the other—

Serling's epilogue is worth quoting at length:

> The tools of conquest do not necessarily come with bombs and explosions and fallout. There are weapons that are simply thoughts, attitudes, prejudices . . . to be found only in the minds of men. For the record, prejudices can kill . . . and suspicion can destroy . . . and a thoughtless, frightened search for a scapegoat has a fallout all of its own—for the children and the children yet unborn. And the pity of it is that these things cannot be confined to the *Twilight Zone*.

One aspect of the episode that is often overlooked, even in Serling's own soliloquy, is that there really is an outside enemy. This is not a flaw in the episode plotline or in Serling's message. Rather, it is a reminder that, while we search for internal enemies, as commonly happened during the Cold War, there is a real external threat that cannot be ignored. The ambiguity of the ending can be the basis of lively classroom discussions.

Media historian J. P. Telotte argues that one reason for the episode's power is its physical setting. Instead of the usual television sets, which could be shoddy and unrealistic, Serling used the MGM backlot for the street scene, something many viewers might recognize from movies and TV shows that celebrated the harmony of post-1945 American life. Thus Serling, as was his style, turns normalcy on its head. In part, the episode is distinctive in that it resembles a film-noir style that was then relatively rare in American television.[25]

CLASS QUESTIONS AND EXERCISES

After watching the film *Them!* and reading Cyndy Hendershot, "Darwin and the Atom," answer the following questions[26]:

1. How does the film reflect concerns about the nuclear age?

2. What role does technology play in this film? In particular, are new or futuristic weapons needed to fight the giant ants, or do the soldiers use existing weapons?
3. How are the government and governmental authority treated in the film? In other words, is the threat of mutant ants the result of a government experiment gone awry?

After reading *The Chrysalids*, answer the following questions:

1. Describe the religious orthodoxy of postapocalyptic Labrador.
2. How is the fear of deviance like the racial ideologies of modern European history?
3. How is Wyndham's novel an expression of the cultural anxieties of post-1945 Britain? Use at least two examples to illustrate your assertion.

Watch "The Monsters Are Due on Maple Street," and then answer the following questions:

1. Analyze what this episode tells us about the anxieties and fears of Americans during the height of the Cold War. In particular, analyze how the fear of alien infiltration turns normal behavior into nefarious actions.
2. Do you see any contemporary parallels to Serling's message about bigotry and scapegoats?
3. How does the actual alien threat use human paranoia as a tactic of conquest?

NOTES

1. See David Seed, *American Science Fiction and the Cold War: Literature and Film* (Chicago: Fitzroy and Dearborn, 1999). For an insightful survey of Soviet and American Cold War films (which unfortunately does not engage with science fiction films), see Tony Shaw and Denise J. Youngblood, *Cinematic Cold War: The American and Soviet Struggle for Hearts and Minds* (Lawrence: University Press of Kansas, 2010).
2. Jack Finney, *The Body Snatchers* (New York: Dell, 1955).
3. J. Hoberman, *An Army of Phantoms: American Movies and the Making of the Cold War* (New York: New Press, 2011), argues that the film can be interpreted as both an anti-Communist and anti-McCarthy message.
4. To date, there is no systematic study of science fiction and the Cold War. Most studies are national or subject-genre in scope. James Chapman and Nicholas Cull, *Projecting Tomorrow: Science Fiction and Popular Culture* (London: I. B. Taurus,

2013), focuses on specific films in the Anglophone world, including some Cold War films. It is a good source for teachers.

5. *Them!*, dir. Gordon Douglas, writ. Ted Sherdeman, Russell S. Hughes, and George Worthing Yates (Warner Bros., 1954); *Twilight Zone*, season 1, episode 22, "The Monsters Are Due on Maple Street," dir. Ron Winston, writ. Rod Serling (aired March 4, 1960, on CBS); and John Wyndham, *The Chrysalids* (1955; New York: New York Review Books, 2008).

6. Carl Abbott, *Frontiers Past and Future: Science Fiction and the American West* (Lawrence: University Press of Kansas, 2006), 1–2.

7. In addition to being broadcast on Turner Classic Movies at least once a year, *Them!* is available as an inexpensive DVD, thus making it easily accessible for class use.

8. For context on the film and as a good reading assignment for students, see Cyndy Hendershot, "Darwin and the Atom: Evolution/Devolution Fantasies in 'The Beast from 20,000 Fathoms,' 'Them!' and 'The Incredible Shrinking Man,'" *Science Fiction Studies* 25, no. 2(July 1998): 319–35.

9. *The Chrysalids* has been in print since its initial publication in 1955. For this chapter, I use John Wyndham, *The Chrysalids* (New York: New York Review Books, 2008). This part of the chapter is adapted from Frederic Krome, Phoebe Reeves, and Greg Loving, "The Concept of the Human in John Wyndham's *The Chrysalids*: Puritanical Imagery, Female Agency, and Theistic Evolution," *Interdisciplinary Humanities* 32, no. 2 (Summer 2015): 52–64.

10. Brian W. Aldiss, "Harris, John Wyndham Parkes Lucas Beynon [*pseud*. John Wyndham] (1903–1969)," *Oxford Dictionary of National Biography*, January 8, 2015, https://doi.org/10.1093/ref:odnb/33728.

11. David Ketterer, "John Wyndham: The Facts of Life Sextet," in *A Companion to Science Fiction*, ed. David See, 375–77 (Malden, MA: Blackwell 2008).

12. David Seed, *Science Fiction: A Very Short Introduction* (New York: Oxford University Press, 2011), 32–34.

13. Roger Luckhurst, *Science Fiction* (Cambridge, UK: Polity, 2005), chap. 6.

14. Wyndham, *Chrysalids*, 5.

15. Wyndham, *Chrysalids*, 16.

16. See Carol Karlsen, *The Devil in the Shape of a Women: Witchcraft in Colonial New England* (New York: Norton, 1998).

17. Wyndham, *Chrysalids*, 5.

18. Wyndham, *Chrysalids*, 64.

19. Wyndham, *Chrysalids*, 88.

20. Wyndham, *Chrysalids*, 36.

21. Wyndham, *Chrysalids*, 38.

22. Kai T. Erickson, *Wayward Puritans: A Study in the Sociology of Deviance* (New York: Wiley, 1966).

23. See, for example, Margot A. Henriksen, *Dr. Strangelove's America: Society and Culture in the Atomic Age* (Berkeley: University of California Press, 1997).

24. *Twilight Zone*, "Monsters Are Due."

25. J. P. Telotte, "In the Cinematic Zone of the *Twilight Zone*," *Science Fiction Film and Television* 3, no. 1 (2010): 10–13.

26. Hendershot, "Darwin and the Atom."

SUGGESTED READING

Chapman, James, and Nicholas Cull. *Projecting Tomorrow: Science Fiction and Popular Culture*. London: I. B. Taurus, 2013.

Henriksen, Margot A. *Dr. Strangelove's America: Society and Culture in the Atomic Age*. Berkeley: University of California Press, 1997.

Krome, Frederic, Phoebe Reeves, and Greg Loving. "The Concept of the Human in John Wyndham's *The Chrysalids*: Puritanical Imagery, Female Agency, and Theistic Evolution," *Interdisciplinary Humanities* 32, no. 2 (Summer 2015): 52–64.

Seed, David. *American Science Fiction and the Cold War: Literature and Film*. Chicago: Fitzroy and Dearborn, 1999.

Shaw, Tony, and Denise J. Youngblood. *Cinematic Cold War: The American and Soviet Struggle for Hearts and Minds*. Lawrence: University Press of Kansas, 2010.

Chapter 6

From *Starship Troopers* to *The Forever War*

This chapter discusses the controversies surrounding Robert Heinlein's *Starship Troopers* and juxtaposes it with Joe Haldeman's *The Forever War*, two examples of military science fiction that defines the period from the early days of the Cold War to the negative reactions to Vietnam.

Classes this lesson can be used for:

- World history
- US history
- US military history
- The Cold War
- Introduction to liberal arts
- Introduction to historical methods

Science fiction texts:

- Joe Haldeman, *The Forever War* (New York: St. Martin's Press, 1974)
- Robert A. Heinlein, *Starship Troopers* (New York: Putnam, 1959)

Since its publication in 1959, Robert Heinlein's *Starship Troopers* has generated a great deal of controversy.[1] Since its publication, critics have regarded it as one of the foundational texts of contemporary military science fiction, while historian Dennis Showalter remarks that, after Heinlein won the Hugo Award for the story in 1960, "critics and reviewers have been apologizing . . . ever since." Those critical of the novel describe it as a "militaristic polemic" in which humanity lives in a neofascist dystopia ruled by a military elite.[2] Even the cover page of the 1987 paperback edition does not shy away from the debate, describing the book as a "controversial classic of military adventure."

A mere fifteen years separate the publication of Heinlein's *Starship Troopers* from Joe Haldeman's *The Forever War*, yet they represent two different epochs in US history.[3] Each book won the Hugo Award for best novel—*The Forever War* in 1976—and they are often regarded as two of the most influential texts of post-1945 military science fiction. As with most science fiction texts, reading them properly can also reveal much about the period in which they were written and as such can serve as a useful teaching tool.

Heinlein was one of the most prominent writers of the so-called golden age of science fiction and published *Starship Troopers* when the military was still held in relatively high esteem by a significant portion of the US population. Haldeman, meanwhile, was a Vietnam veteran whose iconoclastic view of military and political authority fits neatly into the turbulent politics of the late 1960s and early 1970s. Both books remain in print today.[4]

Heinlein's *Starship Troopers* is probably the better-known title to the public, thanks to a big-screen production, several direct-to-video sequels, and an animated series. Yet as with many film adaptations, the cinematic version bears only passing reference to the original novel. It is, however, instructive to discuss a few aspects of the film interpretation, as it helps the instructor understand why the novel was and remains controversial.

The 1997 film version depicts the human "Federation" as a fascist society, even to the point where the soldiers look like they are wearing futuristic versions of World War II Wehrmacht uniforms. In an interview about the film, director Paul Verhoeven argues that he was trying to stay true to Heinlein's vision of that militaristic neofascist society.[5] Thanks to such visuals, the association of Heinlein's novel with militarism and fascism is probably set in concrete in the popular imagination.

Even before its publication, the material and ideas that eventually became Starship Troopers had proven controversial. While Heinlein originally envisioned the novel as an "inquiry into why men fight, investigated as a moral problem," he also insisted that the novel was intended to describe a "libertarian, democratic, almost idyllic utopia—but under wartime conditions and told through the eyes of a young, inexperienced man who had to form his own philosophy under these conditions."[6]

Heinlein's regular editor/publisher rejected the early drafts, saying it was not an adventure story but a social commentary, which meant it was not going to be successful in the young adult market.[7] Still, his name recognition was such that when an editor at G. P. Putnam's Sons heard that a Heinlein manuscript was available, it was accepted, virtually sight unseen.[8] Not surprisingly, the reviews on the book were mixed, and the accusations of militarism and glorification of authoritarianism became part of the discussion almost from the moment of publication.

In its narrative structure, the first third of the book resembles Erich Maria Remarque's classic *All Quiet on the Western Front*.[9] The reader is introduced to the protagonist, Johnnie Rico, a member of the Mobile Infantry (MI) who makes a combat drop on an alien planet, and the fighting suits that turn a regular infantryman into a virtual supersoldier, complete with shoulder-fired mini nukes. After the first battle, the story then turns the clock back, and Rico begins his personal history by saying, "I never really intended to join up."[10] Defying his rich father's demands to the contrary, Rico enlists for battle because finishing military service is a prerequisite for the ability to vote.

What follows is a discourse on the training of a Mobile Infantryman, in which only about one in ten recruits complete basic training, with some fatalities along the way. Rico justifies the brutal regime, saying that "training was made as hard as possible and on purpose" in order to produce the best soldiers.[11] Near the middle of the text, the reader returns to current events (i.e., the Bug War) and then follows a linear narrative to the end.

Shortly after Rico is promoted to corporal, he decides to "go career" and stay in the military even after the war is over. Promoted to sergeant, he is then detached to officer candidates' school, in which Rico must pass a course on history and moral philosophy to stay in the military. Heinlein uses this part of the novel to provide a critique of contemporary society and politics and the importance of military service. After serving as a trainee platoon leader in a bug campaign, Rico is commissioned and posted back to his old unit. The novel ends with him preparing for another mission, leaving open the question if he will be killed in action.

What often strikes the reader of this novel is that, for a foundational text of military science fiction, there are not a lot of depictions of combat. In fact, Heinlein spends a great deal of time using the interstellar confrontation between humanity and its arachnid enemy to discuss political philosophy. Still, Heinlein's depictions of the military as a classless and race-blind institution need to be considered.

Many of the characters have names that either imply a certain ethnicity, such as Juan (Johnnie) Rico, or are ambiguous (such as Sergeant Zim). It is revealed near the end of the novel that Rico himself is from the Philippines. To be fair, in several stories, Heinlein lets his readers assume that the central character is a generic White Anglo-Saxon, only to reveal near the end that they are a person of color.[12]

It is important to remember that Heinlein's novel is a product of the 1950s, when the US military was something of a laboratory of the nation and, according to historian Brian Linn, was very likely the most egalitarian and color-blind institution in the country. Even if some of Heinlein's depictions of weapons seemed outlandish, such as the tactical nukes launched from the fighting suit of a Mobile Infantryman, during the 1950s, the US military trained its soldiers in the potential use of tactical nuclear weapons with the belief that they could limit the use of "atomic weapons" on future battlefields.[13]

When dealing with *Starship Troopers*' political ideology, a good starting place is an article by historian Dennis Showalter. Showalter provides an insightful analysis challenging the characterization of the novel as a "militarist polemic." He argues that, while Heinlein glorifies the military virtues, his narrative does not describe a society in which the military is supreme over the civil leadership. Furthermore, while full citizenship in the Federation, specifically the right to vote and hold office, is limited to veterans, soldiers are not allowed the franchise until after their military service is complete. In addition, while the Mobile Infantry of the story are the elite, tip-of-the-sword-type outfit, they do not enjoy any extra privileges over other groups. In the end, Showalter points out that, even though one of the more controversial political points of Heinlein's novel, that full citizenship is not inherent but a reward for service, is objectionable, the novel is not fascist. Showalter's analysis, which provides a succinct metaclass in applying popular terminology to a novel and why it can often be applied incorrectly, is a good starting point for crafting a lesson plan.

Whereas Heinlein did not base his novel on any specific war, Haldeman's *The Forever War* is a parable about the Vietnam War, both in his personal experiences as a soldier and in the politics that sucked many thousands of Americans into the conflict.[14] Unlike Heinlein's Johnnie Rico, Haldeman was drafted but did not support the war. As with other science fiction texts, Haldeman's story might take place in the future and on other worlds, but in this case, it is based on some very real-world experiences in the jungles of Southeast Asia.

The Forever War is told from the perspective of William Mandella, who is drafted into the United Nations Expeditionary Forces via the Elite Conscription Act of 1996. In the late twentieth century, humanity begins to explore and colonize the galaxy using newly discovered collapsar stars and soon finds themselves at war with an alien race dubbed the Taurans. Along with ninety-nine other men and women of above average physical and mental capacity (minimum IQ of 150), Mandella is part of the first contingent of soldiers to be trained to fight in this interstellar conflict.[15] As part of their training, the draftees are sent to the dwarf planet Charon, where they complete their training and then move onto Stargate, outside the solar system, whose collapsar serves as the major base for all human military operations.

Unlike Heinlein's soldiers, where subjective time on the ship and Earth time are no different, Manella's war requires traveling between the various stars near the speed of light, which means that the subjective time of a soldier is counted in months, while time on Earth passes as decades and centuries.

Because of this, Haldeman's character is best compared to a time traveler, returning from deployment to a world much different from the one he left. Indeed, near the end of the novel, Mandella and his fellow soldiers "played a kind of nostalgia game, comparing the various eras we'd experienced on Earth, and wondering what it would be like in the 700-years-future we were going back to."[16]

There are some similarities between Haldeman's and Heinlein's soldiers. For example, in each, the soldiers are fitted with combat suits that amplify strength and enable movement across hostile environments, including zero atmosphere. In Haldeman's reality, however, the power suits are just as dangerous to the wearer as to the enemy. In addition, where Johnnie Rico's basic training witnesses some fatalities due to accidents, Mandella is told at one point by a superior officer that he would be surprised if only half the training cadre survived the training on Charon. Mandella remarks rather acerbically, "They had spent all that money on us just to kill us in training?"[17]

Mandella fights in several campaigns and is seriously wounded, and all the while, his statistical chance of surviving until the end of his five-year (subjective) hitch starts to approach zero. He eventually rises to the rank of major, mostly due to his seniority, and is put in charge of a strike command to the most distant collapsar known to humanity to serve as bait to lure an enemy attack. Once again, Mandella survives harrowing combat and then leads the remnants of his strike force back to Stargate. Once there, he is informed that he and his soldiers are the last group expected to return and that the war is over.

Indeed, the more-than-one-thousand-year-long war between humanity and the Taurans "had been begun on false premises and only continued because the two races were unable to communicate."[18] In this plot twist, Haldeman is making an obvious connection to the flimsy justifications for escalating American involvement in Vietnam.[19] Despite the rather pessimistic tone of much of the novel, Haldeman manages to come up with a plausibly happy ending for the protagonist.

Joe Haldeman described William Mandella, the narrator of *The Forever War*, as "purely autobiographical." Like his fictional protagonist, Haldeman was something of a time traveler. Drafted into the US Army after he finished his undergraduate degree in 1967, Haldeman was seriously wounded in Vietnam and returned to an America much different from the one he left.[20] In a somewhat biting analogy to the Vietnam War, Haldeman lays most of the blame for his fictional forever war on the human side.

One fundamental difference between Heinlein's and Haldeman's stories is the attitude toward military authority. Heinlein expresses a near reverence for military decision makers, not that he believes they are incapable of making mistakes. For example, the first battle on the enemy's home world Rico says was called Operation Bughouse "but should have been called Operation Madhouse"[21] because everything went wrong. Despite this monumental military screw-up that almost cost humanity the war, Heinlein's hero defends the military leadership: "I am not criticizing General Diennes. I don't know if it is true that he demanded more troops and more support and allowed himself to be overruled by the Sky Marshal-in-Chief—or not. Nor was it any of my business. Furthermore, I doubt if some of the smart second-guessers know all the facts."[22] Rico concludes about the commanding general, "He's radioactive debris on Klendathu and it's much too late to court-martial him, so why talk about it?"[23] This seems an odd defense, for since at least World War I, the US military has exhibited an absolute obsession with studying history, especially military blunders, as a means of not repeating them.[24] Haldeman's Mandella, meanwhile, is acerbically critical of the military hierarchy, not even sparing himself from the absurdities of command decisions. Even when he is promoted to major, he is ambiguous about his authority, especially when he discovers that most of his troops hate him.

From the earliest review of Haldeman's book, it was juxtaposed with Heinlein's. For example, *Kirkus Reviews* described *The Forever War* as the "opposite of the one Heinlein glorified in *Starship Troopers* . . . bloody, cruel, and meaningless. This is a splendid, thoughtful adventure."[25] Interestingly, Haldeman rejected the comparison, saying that, while his novel was antiwar, "it wasn't an 'answer' to Starship Troopers, as some people claimed. Novels aren't conversations. I liked Starship Troopers for what it was, a quickly written didactic novel with some great action scenes." He also said that Heinlein told him that he liked *The Forever War* so much he read it three times.[26]

Like all subgenres, military science fiction is a niche market; however, that niche market is rather large. It is interesting to see the reaction of students to these two novels, which, like the authors themselves, is shaped by personal experience and what period of US history they were born into. The current generation, seeing some of their own versions of the forever war finally coming to an end, might have a different attitude toward the military than those of the Vietnam generation. At the least, the current generation might revere the common soldier and not think much of the military brass.

CLASS QUESTIONS AND EXERCISES

Read Robert A. Heinlein's *Starship Troopers* and Dennis Showalter's "Heinlein's *Starship Troopers*," then answer the following questions[27]:

1. Does Johnnie Rico live in a militaristic or a fascist society? Use specific examples to illustrate your assertions.

2. Does the novel glorify war or glorify the military or both?

Read Joe Haldeman's *The Forever War*, and then answer the following questions:

1. What is Haldeman's attitude toward military authority?
2. Analyze the gender roles in the novel, and compare them to contemporary attitudes toward women in the military.

A longer assignment: Have the students read Heinlein's *Starship Troopers* and then compare the military hardware and tactics of the Mobile Infantry to the US military of the 1950s. Do they see any similarities?

A PHOTO ESSAY ON THE ATOMIC BATTLEFIELD

One of my own teachers once remarked, "Reality sometimes catches up to science fiction." Yet as this volume illustrates, history is often the secret source for science fiction writers. When considering such novels as Heinlein's *Starship Troopers*, the instructor would do well to consider whether the tactics of the Mobile Infantry described by Heinlein are a repeat of World War II paratrooper operations or an example of innovation fueled by technological advances. Likewise, it can be an interesting exercise to consider the broader context of US military doctrine in the era when Heinlein wrote the novel.

It is an old truism that soldiers often plan on refighting the last war. While containing some grains of truth, an examination of the US Army in the aftermath of World War II reveals a more complex picture. As the Cold War developed, many American military planners relied on the lessons of World War II, in which massive aerial bombing destroyed enemy infrastructure, while vast ground forces annihilated the enemy's army. Using these historical lessons, the assumption of military planners was that the next war with the Soviet Union would follow a similar path of mayhem; this came to be known as the general war concept. In the general war, a massive aerial assault by the air force and Navy using nuclear weapons would destroy the enemy in relatively quick time, leaving little for ground forces to do. Of course, the Soviets, it was assumed, were engaged in the same type of planning.[28]

After 1945, the US Army was faced with severe budget cuts, along with the challenge of the massive demobilization of troops and a sense (at least among some army leaders) that a new doctrine had to be developed for the next war, and soon. Failure to make the army relevant in the nuclear age, it was feared, meant that the army would lose out to the navy and the air force in the court of public opinion, as well as in congressional authorizations.

This is the Army's famous atomic cannon, which brings mobile atomic artillery to the battlefield. This gigantic weapon, despite its size, is readily moved along highways or even cross-country by two motorized tractors, one at each end of the weapon.

The gun is power-operated for elevation and ammunition feed. On-site electric generators driven by gasoline engines permit operation without additional engineering support. Maximum range is 18 miles and high explosive ammunition can be fired in addition to atomic shells. In fact, conventional projectiles would be used to zero in on a target before cutting loose the M65's nuclear punch.

Long-range, atomic firepower, mobility and reliable, all-weather operation give this gun maximum capability for destroying the heaviest enemy fortifications and defense positions.

Figure 6.1: 280 mm Howitzer capable of firing a tactical nuclear warhead. The desirability of using small-yield nuclear weapons on the modern battlefield was widely discussed among policy makers during the early Cold War. *Courtesy of Will Eisner, A Pictorial Arsenal of America's Combat Weapons (New York: Sterling, 1960), 67.*

Figure 6.2: "Honest John" and "Little John" were rockets (they lacked the guidance systems of a missile). The logic was to provide tactical nuclear firepower for the modern battlefield. *Courtesy of Will Eisner, A Pictorial Arsenal of America's Combat Weapons (New York: Sterling, 1960), 90–91.*

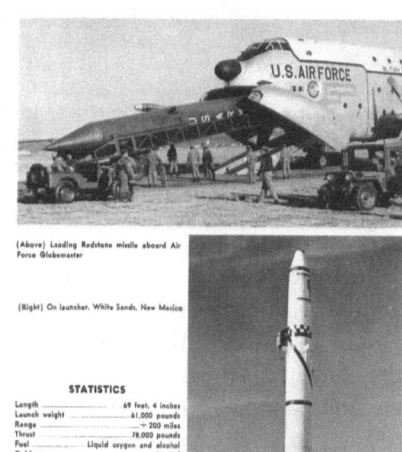

Figure 6.3: The design of the Redstone ballistic missile (in service 1958–1964) was based on the German V-2. *Courtesy of Will Eisner, A Pictorial Arsenal of America's Combat Weapons (New York: Sterling, 1960), 86–87.*

Chapter 6

STATISTICS
Not available

The Davy Crockett is an expansion of the Army's recoilless rifles, and is designed to bring atomic warhead capability to the front-line infantry. Portable enough to be mounted on a jeep or hand-carried by a three-man team, this weapon is designed to fit into the new tactics which atomic warfare introduces into military thinking. It can deliver an atomic shell powerful enough for effective use and yet with a radioactive fallout radius small enough so that the troops using the weapon can maneuver without danger of radiation. It can fire a conventional warhead as well, and operates in combat from either a light or heavy tripod, and from vehicles such as jeeps, armored carriers or "mechanical mules."

Figure 6.4: The Davy Crockett was intended to provide US soldiers, particularly paratroopers, with nuclear capabilities. Officially, it was deployed between 1961 and 1971; however, the nuclear warheads were removed from service in the mid-1960s. *Courtesy of Will Eisner, A Pictorial Arsenal of America's Combat Weapons (New York: Sterling, 1960), 39.*

In opposition to the concept of the general war, which could lead to the annihilation of all life on Earth, some military planners worked to develop a doctrine for the limited use of nuclear weapons within a combat zone; thus, the concept of the atomic battlefield was born. In this hypothesis, small tactical units armed with low-yield, portable nuclear weapons would limit the use of nuclear weapons to a self-contained combat zone. By the mid-1950s, the army had tried to develop and test what were called tactical nuclear weapons, which could be fired either by heavy guns or even hand-carried mortars.

In 1960, Will Eisner, mostly famous for his work in graphic illustration, did a picture book entitled *A Pictorial Arsenal of America's Combat Weapons*, and while it covered all branches of the US military, it also contained examples of the proposed weapons for the atomic battlefield.[29] The illustrations listed here come from Eisner's book and can be used to juxtapose the imagery of nuclear weapons on the battlefield described in Heinlein's *Starship Troopers* with some actual weapons under development (and never used) in that period. How realistic was the notion of limited use of nuclear weapons for the battlefield? Can you identify flaws in the theory of tactical use of nuclear weapons?

NOTES

1. Robert A. Heinlein, *Starship Troopers* (New York: Putnam, 1959).
2. Dennis E. Showalter, "Heinlein's *Starship Troopers*: An Exercise in Rehabilitation," *Extrapolation* 16, no. 2 (1974): 113.
3. Joe Haldeman, *The Forever War* (New York: St. Martin's Press, 1974).
4. While Heinlein's texts remain unchanged, the 1997 edition of Haldeman's book contains a substantively revised section on the protagonist's return to an early-twenty-first-century Earth.
5. For a sample of the various interviews Verhoeven did about the film, see Chris O'Falt, "Paul Verhoeven Slams 'Starship Troopers' Remake, Says It'll Be a Fascist Update Perfect for a Trump Presidency," IndieWire, November 16, 2016, https://www.indiewire.com/2016/11/paul-verhoeven-slams-starship-troopers-remake-fascist-update-perfect-trump-presidency-1201747155/.
6. William H. Patterson Jr., *Robert A. Heinlein: In Dialogue with His Century*, vol. 2: *1948–1988: The Man Who Learned Better* (New York: Tor Books, 2014), 162–63.
7. Patterson, *Robert A. Heinlein*, 166.
8. Patterson, *Robert A. Heinlein*, 173.
9. Erich Maria Remarque, *All Quiet on the Western Front*, trans. A. W. Wheen (London: G. P. Putnam's Sons, 1929).
10. Heinlein, *Starship Troopers*, 13.
11. Heinlein, *Starship Troopers*, 45.
12. Christopher Nuttall, "The Quiet Diversity of Robert Anson Heinlein," Mad Genius Club, January 3, 2018, https://madgeniusclub.com/2018/01/03/the-quiet-diversity-of-robert-anson-heinlein-by-christopher-nuttall/.
13. For a discussion of the US Army of this era, see Brian McAllister Linn, *Elvis's Army: Cold War GIs and the Atomic Battlefield* (Cambridge, MA: Harvard University Press, 2016).
14. David M. Higgins, "New Wave Science Fiction and the Vietnam War," in *The Cambridge History of Science Fiction*, ed. Gerry Canavan and Eric Carl Link, 420–24 (New York: Cambridge University Press, 2019).
15. I use the revised 1997 edition of the book, which contains biographical and critical material that helps provide context for the novel.
16. Haldeman, *Forever War*, 257.
17. Haldeman, *Forever War*, 13.
18. Haldeman, *Forever War*, 261.
19. For an analysis of the Vietnam War that fits well with Haldeman's worldview, see John Prado, *Vietnam: The History of an Unwinnable War, 1945–1975* (Lawrence: University Press of Kansas 2009).

20. Andrew Liptak, "Interview with Joe Haldeman," *Andrew Liptak* (blog), November 13, 2014, https://www.andrewliptak.com/blog/2014/11/13/interview-with-joe-haldeman.

21. Heinlein, *Starship Troopers*, 107.

22. Ibid.

23. Ibid.

24. Information about the American military and its attitude toward the study of history comes from my interactions with scholars at a number of institutions and the annual meeting of the Society for Military History. In addition to the Command and General Staff College in Kansas, which routinely holds history seminars on lessons learned from military mistakes, the US Army Heritage and Education Center in Carlisle, Pennsylvania, is dedicated to the study of military history. The US Navy runs similar institutions.

25. *Kirkus Reviews*, "Review of *The Forever War* by Joe Haldeman," November 1, 1974.

26. Liptak, "Interview with Joe Haldeman."

27. Showalter, "Heinlein's *Starship Troopers*."

28. This section is based on Linn, *Elvis's Army*, chap. 3.

29. Will Eisner, *A Pictorial Arsenal of America's Combat Weapons* (New York: Sterling, 1960). An introduction by retired major general J. B. Medaris, the former chief of the US Army Ordnance Missile Command, emphasizes the importance of bringing new weapons to the fore.

SUGGESTED READING

Eisner, Will. *A Pictorial Arsenal of America's Combat Weapons*. New York: Sterling, 1960.

Linn, Brian McAllister. *Elvis's Army: Cold War GIs and the Atomic Battlefield*. Cambridge, MA: Harvard University Press, 2016.

Prado, John. *Vietnam: The History of an Unwinnable War, 1945–1975*. Lawrence: University Press of Kansas, 2009.

Showalter, Dennis E. "Heinlein's *Starship Troopers*: An Exercise in Rehabilitation." *Extrapolation* 16, no. 2 (1974): 113–24.

Chapter 7

From *Dune* to *The Ministry for the Future*

Environmentalism in Science Fiction

This chapter looks at the rise of environmental consciousness in science fiction and considers how such science fiction authors as Kim Stanley Robinson use novels as a bully pulpit for environmental issues.

Classes this lesson can be used for:

- Modern world history
- History of ideas
- Environmental history
- Interdisciplinary studies
- Global challenges

Science fiction films and texts:

- *Dune: Part One*, directed by Denis Villeneuve, written by Jon Spaihts, Denis Villeneuve, and Eric Roth (Warner Bros., 2021)
- *Dune: Part Two*, directed by Denis Villeneuve, written by Denis Villeneuve, Jon Spaihts, and Frank Herbert (Warner Bros., 2024)
- Frank Herbert, *Dune* (Philadelphia: Chilton Books, 1965)
- Marge Piercy, *He, She, and It: A Novel* (New York: Knopf, 1991)
- Kim Stanley Robinson, *The Ministry for the Future* (New York: Orbit, 2020)

Environmental themes are common in science fiction. Catastrophic climate change can serve as a useful setting for authors to engage with questions about human morality, the price of survival, or how technological adaptation affects human behavior. For example, Sydney Fowler Wright's *Deluge* begins with the oceans rising and destroying civilization.[1] The plotline, however, focuses on how the survivors in the British Isles, deprived of the benefits of the industrial world and modern government, alter their moral codes to survive in a barbaric world.[2] Interestingly, the story was adapted into an RKO movie in 1933, which set the events on the East Coast of the United States.[3] Interestingly, in most of these stories, the environmental change or climate disaster is a plot device for the story. To put it another way, the issue of climate change is not the purpose of the story, just something that serves as the backdrop for character development.

While the roots of science fiction's engagement with environmentalism are complex, the increasing interest in the subject owes a great deal to the publication of Rachel Carson's *Silent Spring* in 1962, a book that is credited with moving environmental concerns into the mainstream of political discourse.[4] In fact, Carson's first chapter, "A Fable for Tomorrow," uses a narrative style comparable to science fiction storytelling to describe a bucolic small town whose symbiotic relationship with nature is destroyed by chemical pesticides. Although the town is an amalgamation of many different real locations, it serves to center a budding environmental catastrophe caused by human action as the fundamental theme of the book: "The people had done it to themselves."[5]

This lament of anthropogenic environmental disaster became a common motif in science iction stories throughout the 1960s.[6] A prime example of this is found in the original *Planet of the Apes* film.[7] In perhaps the most iconic moment in 1960s American science fiction, Taylor the astronaut (played by Charlton Heston) discovers the remains of the Statue of Liberty along a seacoast. It turns out that the desolate world he thought was an alien planet is in fact a post-nuclear-war planet Earth (c. 3978 AD). His final lines resonate with Carson's point: "We finally really did it. You maniacs! You blew it up!"[8]

The emergence of environmental consciousness was also a part of the 1960s movement in science fiction known as the new wave. The new wave was marked by experimentation in narrative form, an exploration of the nature of human consciousness, and (in a genre often noted for dissent from societal norms) an aggressive form of anti-imperialism and distrust of authority.[9]

In addition to stories that focus on environmental catastrophe or the danger of climate change, a new subgenre within science fiction emerged that the *Encyclopedia of Science Fiction* calls the "planetary romance" story; a planetary romance is one in which the "world itself encompasses—and generally survives—the tale which fitfully illuminates it."[10] Combine portrayals of the planet as a character with the developing environmental consciousness among science fiction authors, and we get the novel *Dune*.[11]

Frank Herbert (1920–1986) was a journalist with an interest in environmentalism and Zen meditation, along with a streak of libertarianism in his politics. The idea for *Dune*, perhaps the most famous and best-selling science fiction book of all time, came out of his research for an article on West Coast sand dunes and the government's efforts to control them with imported grasses.[12] Although the article was never written, the information he gathered found its way into the novel.[13]

While *Dune* won the Nebula Award and was tied for the Hugo Award, initially it was not a best-seller; indeed, for a few years, it appealed primarily to members of the counterculture and only gradually moved into the mainstream.[14] In 1984, it was adapted into a film version by director David Lynch, an interpretation that underwhelmed critics and science fiction fans alike. A SyFy miniseries was broadcast in 2000, and another film version was released in two parts, in 2021 and 2024. Herbert wrote four sequels, and after his death in 1986, his son Brian expanded the *Dune* franchise even further.[15]

Science fiction historian Adam Roberts argues that the "most obvious aspect of *Dune* is that it is an environmental novel."[16] The planet, officially known as Arrakis, is a vast desert, where water is a precious commodity. The indigenous inhabitants—the Fremen—are alternatively exploited and hunted by imperialist powers, who only value the planet for its unique natural resource, the spice melange. Dune is the only place in the universe where the spice exists. Not only does the spice have medical benefits, but it also enables Navigators of the Spacing Guild to enter into a trancelike state that enables them to safely plot the path between planetary systems, thus making interstellar travel and commerce possible.

The Imperium in Herbert's book is neofeudal in structure, with a rigid caste system. Paradoxically, the civilization is scientifically advanced—in addition to space travel, it features sophisticated mechanical equipment for flying on planets—and yet has a religious abhorrence of "thinking machines" (i.e., computers). One of the interesting aspects of Herbert's world building is the backstory to the events of the novel. For example, he provides a glossary titled "Terminology of the Imperium" that explains terms and references in the text.

While this sometimes interrupts the narrative flow as readers stop to consult the terminology, it also fills out the story.[17] Thus we learn that hundreds of years before the events of *Dune*, which is set in the two hundredth century, a religious crusade called the Butlerian Jihad had destroyed computers, and now there is a religious prohibition expressed in their sacred text: "thou shalt not make a machine in the likeness of the human mind."[18]

In addition to the "Terminology," Herbert provides appendixes on the ecology and religion of Dune, biographical sketches of a few major characters, and a description of the goals and methods of a mystical order known as the Bene Gesserit Sisterhood. These addenda are as fascinating as the story itself.

Along with these supplemental reading, each chapter begins with a passage purportedly written by the emperor's daughter Princess Irulan, which places the events of the novel into the wider political history of the Imperium.

The primary narrative follows the main protagonist, Paul Atreides, a scion of a noble house, whose mother is a member of the Bene Gesserit order. By imperial decree, Paul's father, Duke Leto, is ordered to assume the fief of Arrakis, supplanting their mortal enemies of House Harkonnen. While the blood feud between the two houses goes back centuries, the majority of the narrative takes place on Arrakis and integrates environmentalism within the plotline. So rather than being a backdrop to a political story, the events that shape Paul Atreides' life choices make sense only in the context of the environmental story.

Betrayed by one of his own men and targeted by the emperor, who provides the Harkonnens with additional troops, the Atreides are overwhelmed, and Duke Leto and most of his men are killed. Paul and his mother, Lady Jessica, escape into the desert, where they are found by the Fremen.

Herbert depicts the Fremen as direct, honest, and egalitarian. They are also practical; their leader, Stilgar, initially thinks Jessica is too old to adapt to the ways of the desert and should be killed so her bodily water can be claimed for Fremen use. Stilgar changes his mind when Jessica demonstrates her ability in hand-to-hand combat and subdues him with ease. Although now accepted into the tribe, Jessica expresses a fear that she and Paul might be betrayed. The Fremens' honesty and integrity is juxtaposed with the corruption of the Imperium when Stilgar responds, "Out here, woman, we carry no paper for contracts. We make no evening promises to be broken at dawn. When a man says a thing, that's his contract."[19]

Herbert's depiction of the Fremens' honorable behavior, the lack of conspicuous consumption in daily life, and the intense commitment to the community could easily be confused with the Kiplingesque vision of the noble savage. Paul and his mother, however, discover that the Fremen are not simple natives, but an ecologically sophisticated people engaged in a covert project to change the very climate of Dune. The Fremen have established water caches all over the planet, are anchoring the sand dunes with plants, and are slowly changing the environment. It is a project that will take centuries to complete. Paul's arrival in the Fremen world upsets this plan. Without him, the Fremen are fierce and courageous fighters, able to meet the best soldiers of the Imperium one on one and beat them. Paul provides the leadership to give their resistance a wider strategy.

Herbert also combines his environmental story with mystical religious concepts based on his study of Zen. For example, the novel does not attempt to explain the technology of space travel. All we are told is that the spice enables the Guild Navigators to find safe pathways, with no detailed plot device beyond the importance of the spice. As for the Bene Gesserit, they are engaged in a centuries-long eugenics experiment to breed a male messianic figure who can see into the past, present, and future simultaneously.

The Fremen, meanwhile, are described as Zensunni, a fusion of Islam and Zen Buddhism, whose religion contains a belief in a messianic figure who will lead them to paradise. Furthermore, the Sisterhood has prepared the Fremen to accept the idea that this messianic figure would come from off-world and have a Bene Gesserit mother. So Paul's presence on Arrakis will quickly trigger a religious war, a jihad, among the Fremen.

Of particular interest to the instructor who would like to engage with the environmental issues is "Appendix One: The Ecology of Dune." In this section, Herbert provides much of the backstory to the development of the Fremens' ecological consciousness. One such use for the source is to consider how it reflects the development of environmentalism in the post-1945 world.

MARGE PIERCY: ENVIRONMENTALISM AND DYSTOPIA

In addition to environmentalism, new-wave science fiction (1960s and '70s) promoted experimentation with narrative form and content and was a major influence on the development of the cyberpunk subgenre in the 1980s. Science fiction author Bruce Sterling describes cyberpunk as juxtaposing technological change with dystopian imagination in a narrative that mixes "lowlife and high tech," scenarios.[20] In 1991, Marge Piercy (b. 1936) combined cyberpunk and environmental science fiction in her novel *He, She, and It*. Although Piercy's is not explicitly identified as a science fiction author, her novel *Women on the Edge of Time* (1976) is considered both a feminist classic and a foray into speculative fiction.[21]

In typical cyberpunk fashion, Piercy describes the mid-twenty-first century as a high-tech world where synthetic organs are grown for people who need transplants and cybernetic implants enable an individual to have a direct hook-up to the virtual reality of the World Wide Web. Yet this Earth is also ravaged by the cataclysmic effects of climate change. The collapse of the ozone layer has led to destructive UV radiation scorching the grain-producing regions of the world, turning them into deserts, and as the temperature has increased, the ice caps have melted and the ocean level has risen, drowning the coastal cities.

There is no working central government in the United States. Multinational corporations have taken over parts of the country and built enclaves (the Multis), where the privileged work and live, protected from the harsh UV radiation by giant canopies. Most of the rest of the population provide day labor for the Multis while living in the Glop, the degraded remains of cities where gangs rule; diseases are common; and life is nasty, brutish, and usually short. The Multis periodically wage war against competitors by sending assassins (called Razors) into virtual reality to "burn" (i.e., destroy) the minds of those working in the Web.

The storyline follows Shira Shipman, an employee of one of the Multis who has lost custody of her son to her ex-husband and whose work is denigrated by her superiors. Shira decides to quit her job and move back to her childhood home to reunite with Malkah, the grandmother who raised her. Shira returns to Tikvah (Hebrew for *hope*), a Jewish free town on the East Coast of the United States. Like other free towns, Tikvah exists precariously between the Multis and the Glop. Tikvah specializes in producing chimaera, virtual security software for various clients around the world. In its society, governmental structure, and economy, the town resembles an idealized Israeli kibbutz.

The action of *He, She, and It* is set in two eras and places, mid-twenty-first century United States and sixteenth-century Prague, and it follows the parallel stories of the Golem of Prague (sixteenth century) and Yod (the tenth letter in the Hebrew alphabet), a twenty-first century cyborg, or, in other words, a modern-day golem. The original golem is the creation of the mystic Rabbi Loew of Prague, known as the Maharal (an acronym for "Our Teacher, Rabbi Loew"). In the traditional story, the Golem is fashioned from clay by Rabbi Loew and animated through mystical Kabbalistic incantations. The Golem, called Joseph, is mute and is tasked with protecting the Jews of Prague during a time of crisis.

Yod, meanwhile, is a hybrid creature made of cybernetic and synthetic parts, has consciousness, can speak, and is anatomically male, down to his working sexual organs. He is also tasked with protecting the modern-day Jewish community of Tikvah during a time of crisis, either in person or in virtual reality, as a defender against the Multis' Razor assassins. Despite consciousness, Yod does not yet understand how to be human. Yod's creator has tasked Malkah and Shira with teaching the cyborg the nuances of human emotions. The use of the name Yod is significant, as in Kabbalist circles it is shorthand for the name of God.[22]

While Shira spends time introducing Yod to the world, including sexual contact, Malkah chooses to teach Yod by telling him the story of the Golem of Prague. Malkah's story, however, differs from the traditional narrative in that Joseph, the Golem of Prague, is depicted as having the ability to speak and having consciousness. In Malkah's storyline, Rabbi Loew's widowed daughter Chava is Joseph's instructor in how to be human. Thus, the parallel storylines intersect. Yod's quest to understand humanity, indeed, to become more human himself, raises interesting questions about the nature of consciousness and artificial intelligence for classroom discussion.

Piercy's novel operates on several levels as a historical source. Written in the early days of the World Wide Web, Piercy's description of what she calls "the base" (i.e., the virtual-reality world) is not an accurate prognostication of technological developments. She does, however, capture the essence of how information and its control play a prominent part in the modern world economy. One of the novel's characters, Shira's mother, Rivka, is an "information pirate" who "liberates"[23] knowledge. For example, Rivka has stolen the process for making a vaccine for one of the innumerable diseases killing people in the Glop, thereby enabling it to be widely and cheaply produced. Such activities have made Rivka an enemy of the Multis with a price on her head.

The villains of Piercy's world are the Multis, who control information, the distribution of the food supply, and thus jobs. The Multi for whom Shira had worked discovers Yod's existence and decides they wanted to obtain the secrets of his creation. It turns out that Shira losing custody of her son is part of a plan to force her out of her job, with the expectation that she would return to Tikvah. Once she learns details of Yod's construction, the Multi plans on kidnapping her and extracting the information from her by force. Thanks to Rivka, Malkah, and Yod, Shira regains custody of her son, and the Multi's plan fails. In the end, Yod sacrifices himself to save Tikvah, the denizens of the Glop rise in rebellion against the Multis, and the potential for positive change is within reach.

Although it is often used as a framing device for scenes, the environment plays an important part in the novel. For example, when Shira and Yod swim in the ocean, Piercy refers to the detritus of the industrial world in the smell of oil in the water and the ruins of now-submerged towns. The lamentation of what was lost in the ecological disasters is a constant and painful backdrop to the story. As Shira remarks, "No one before the twenty-first century had ever loved flowers and fruiting trees and little birds and the simple beauty of green leaves as those who lived after the Famine, for whom they were precious and rare and always endangered."[24]

Despite the dystopian imagery, there is also hope. Every year, citizens of Tikvah are required to go out into the sand dunes and plant trees, bushes, and grass as part of the effort to reclaim the planet. Thus, the Jewish town attempts to fulfill the ancient Jewish commitment of Tikkun Olam (repairing the world). As in the case of the denizens of Arrakis, it will take a long time to fix the broken world.

Chapter 7

THE SCIENCE FICTION AUTHOR AS ACTIVIST: *THE MINISTRY FOR THE FUTURE*

There is nothing unique in a science fiction author expressing strong political opinions or, indeed, using their literary skills to promote political causes. The career of Jerry Pournelle (1933–2017) provides an interesting case study. After serving in Korea, he earned a PhD in political science and then moved to work on defense projects in the aerospace industry before becoming a full-time writer. Science fiction author and literary historian Thomas Disch argues that, by the 1970s, Pournelle was "SF's premier cold warrior."[25]

From 1982 through 1990, Pournelle edited a ten-volume series entitled *There Will Be War*, which contains not only reprints of military science fiction originally published in magazines but also essays on military technology, some specially commissioned for the series. Although the early volumes contain stories by such left-of-center authors as Philip K. Dick, later volumes trend toward a much more conservative line. Indeed, in the latter volumes, many contributors were supporters of President's Reagan's Strategic Defense Initiative (SDI).[26]

In 1980, Pournelle was also one of the organizers of the Citizens Advisory Council on National Space Policy, which contained a number of science fiction writers and dealt with such issues as the militarization of space.[27] Indeed, Pournelle later recounted, "We were, after all, trying to form bold new concepts, and SF people's imagination were needed."[28] Interestingly, science fiction author Norman Spinrad claims that part of President Reagan's speech on SDI was in fact written by Pournelle, an assertion the latter denied.[29]

Kim Stanley Robinson (b. 1952) also believes that science fiction can be used as an agent of change, though his politics are clearly to the left of someone like Pournelle. Robinson, who describes his politics as Democratic Socialist, argues that capitalism and wealth inequality are the primary drivers of global climate change.[30] While the new wave often turned the old paradigm of the hero-scientist on its head and made them the villains, Robinson returns to a more traditional view of science and technology and their potential to solve problems. Although he is not naïve about the negative potential of technology, he nonetheless seems to accept the importance of experts in the development of rational conservation policies.[31] In *New York 2140*, for example, rampant capitalism has led to the melting of the polar ice caps, and a fifty-foot rise in the ocean levels has flooded much of Manhattan.[32] The city is now divided into two primary regions. Lower Manhattan is likened to Venice, indeed, that section of the city is referred to as Super Venice, by its inhabitants. The poor live on the upper floors of old skyscrapers, where some have to scrounge in the wreckage of Lower Manhattan to survive, while the affluent live in purpose-built skyscrapers in Upper Manhattan. Robinson purposely chooses the near future for his setting, for he believes that the city would be recognizable to the reader. He also believes it is important for the science of his stories to appear realistic, so the story appeals to the reader.[33]

The role of capitalism as driver of climate catastrophe is similarly explicit in *The Ministry for the Future*, which might be his most influential book to date.[34] The novel begins in India in the near future, where temperatures have risen to record highs and have killed millions over a few days. Frank May, an American aid worker, is one of the few survivors of the heat wave and spends much of the book looking for means of coping with his PTSD and survivor's guilt. He eventually moves to Zurich, where he alternates between helping to feed and provide medical aid to climate refugees from the global South and lashing out at those whom he feels are responsible for the ongoing climate catastrophe.

At one point, he briefly kidnaps Irishwoman Mary Murphy, a United Nations official. Mary is the head of a United Nations agency, the Ministry for the Future, whose charge is to advocate for future generations and seek ways to enforce the various climate treaties that nations ratify but do not implement. The stories of Frank and Mary intersect at various points in the more than one hundred short chapters in the novel, but neither character is particularly three-dimensional. Rather, it is the planet and the ongoing global challenges of climate change that are the focus. Some chapters digress into discussions of the economic systems that govern international commerce and concomitantly promote policies that guarantee global climate change.

Interwoven between Mary's efforts to change international monetary policy (among other policies) and Frank's mental crisis, Robinson proposes possible solutions to climate change. Some are international in scope, such as the creation of a "carbon coin" that would be paid to states, businesses, or even individuals who sequester carbon. Interestingly, many other solutions are done on the local or regional level, without any central planning agency. Some are rather ingenious engineering concepts, such as siphoning melting ice water from deep in Antarctica to the surface, where it can refreeze, thereby reenforcing the ice sheet.

Such suggestions fulfill Robinson's mandate that the science in his science fiction must appear practical. One suggestion harks back to the early days of flight, where lighter-than-air ships—zeppelins—were believed to be the future of aviation. Such machines could replace the fossil fuel–burning jet engines that contribute to carbon emissions. The devotee of science fiction will likely find this suggestion intriguing because, in many steampunk stories, which reimagine the impact of the Victorian age on technology, the zeppelin beats out the airplane as the preferred method of aerial transportation.[35]

Robinson has long advocated for a change in human behavior as a means of saving the planet. For example, in a 2018 article in the *Guardian*, Robinson reports that the Global Footprint Network estimated that every year the world exhausts its renewable resources by August and after that have to use nonrenewable resources. The metaphor Robinson uses is, "Eating the seed corn," or "stealing from future generations."[36] In addition, the burning of fossil fuels and the general carbon footprint of modern civilization are among the primary factors driving global climate change.

Robinson argues that the only long-term hope for humanity is to empty half the planet and move the population to megacities. Robinson's argument is worth quoting at length:

> [L]eave about half the Earth's surface mostly free of humans, so wild plants and animals can live there unimpeded as they did for so long before humans arrived. Same with the oceans, by the way; about a third of our food comes from the sea, so the seas have to be healthy too. At a time when there are far more people alive than ever before, this plan might sound strange, even impossible. But it isn't. With people already leaving countrysides all over the world to move to the cities, big regions are emptier of humans than they were a century ago, and getting emptier still. Many villages now have populations of under a thousand, and continue to shrink as most of the young people leave. If these places were redefined (and repriced) as becoming usefully empty, there would be caretaker work for some, gamekeeper work for others, and the rest could go to the cities and get into the main swing of things.[37]

Robinson goes on to argue that, if agriculture could be made carbon-neutral and if a carbon-negative policy, which would drain carbon out of the atmosphere, could be implemented, then the health of the planet can be restored. Robinson's article, in conjunction with at least one of his novels, can provide a very useful starting point for either classroom discussion or for longer student projects on how to solve the challenges of global climate change.

CLASS QUESTIONS AND EXERCISES

After reading Frank Herbert's *Dune*, answer the following questions:

1. Analyze the political organization of the Imperium. In particular, analyze the roles of the Space Guild, the Bene Gesserit, and the Landsraat.
2. The Fremen: freedom fighters for ecological justice or crazed jihadists?
3. Analyze the ecology of Dune and the Fremen plan to change the desert. Does it appear feasible?

After reading Marge Piercy's *He, She, and It*, answer the following questions:

1. Piercy's book tells the parallel story of the Golem of Prague (sixteenth century) and Yod (twenty-first century). The traditional golem story is told from the perspective of Rabbi Loew (i.e., a man), and the golem is mute and was created to defend the Jews of Prague. How does Piercy's telling differ from the traditional image?
2. Look up the definition of *cyberpunk*.[38] How is the Piercy book an example of the genre? How do the character of Yod and the type of mechanical enhancements that modify people in the story raise questions about what it means to be human?
3. Describe the environmental catastrophe that Piercy envisions in the novel. Does her image of the future differ from the imagery in *Things to Come* (and other futuristic settings you've investigated)?

Read Kim Stanley Robinson's *The Ministry for the Future* and "Empty Half the Earth of Its Humans."[39] Then answer the following questions:

1. Robinson argues that the future of humanity lies in cities. What arguments does he present for this path as the only viable one for humanity?
2. What major infrastructure challenges would we have to overcome to create such a future (e.g., what water and energy issues would have to be solved)? What political challenges do you foresee in creating megacities?
3. Do the political and infrastructure goals presented in *The Ministry for the Future* seem practical? Explain your answer using specific examples.

NOTES

1. Sydney Fowler Wright, *Deluge* (London: F. Wright, 1927).
2. Available in a modern edition in the Wesleyan University Press series Early Classics of Science Fiction. See Sydney Fowler Wright, *Deluge*, ed. Brian Stableford (Middletown, CT: Wesleyan University Press, 2003).
3. *Deluge*, dir. Felix E. Feist, writ. S. Fowler Wright, John F. Goodrich, and Warren Duff (RKO, 1933), https://www.youtube.com/watch?v=CnUVWmtaqHE.
4. Rachel Carson, *Silent Spring* (Boston: Houghton Mifflin, 1962). See Linda Lear, *Rachel Carson: Witness for Nature* (New York: Henry Holt, 1997), 407–8.
5. Carson, *Silent Spring*, 3.
6. This paragraph draws heavily from Rebecca Evans, "New Wave Science Fiction and the Dawn of the Environmental Movement," in *The Cambridge History of Science Fiction*, ed. Gerry Caravan and Eric Carl Link, 436–37 (New York: Cambridge University Press, 2019).

7. *Planet of the Apes*, dir. Franklin J. Schaffner, writ. Michael Wilson, Rod Serling, and Pierre Boulle (Twentieth Century Fox, 1968).

8. "Planet of the Apes (5/5) Movie Clip—Statue of Liberty (1968) HD," video, 2:42, August 17, 2015, https://www.youtube.com/watch?v=mDLS12_a-fk.

9. For analysis of the new wave, see part II of Gerry Canavan and Eric Carl Link, eds., *The Cambridge History of Science Fiction* (New York: Cambridge University Press, 2019), 321–78.

10. Encyclopedia of Science Fiction, "Planetary Romance," December 4, 2013, https://sf-encyclopedia.com/entry/planetary_romance.

11. Frank Herbert, *Dune* (Philadelphia: Chilton Books, 1965).

12. Best Sci Fi Books, "The Bestselling Science Fiction Books of All Time," November 28, 2021, https://best-sci-fi-books.com/the-bestselling-science-fiction-books-of-all-time/.

13. Encyclopedia of Science Fiction, "Herbert, Frank," September 12, 2022, https://sf-encyclopedia.com/entry/herbert_frank.

14. Hari Kunzru, "Dune 50 Years On: How a Science Fiction Novel Changed the World," *Guardian*, July 3, 2015, https://www.theguardian.com/books/2015/jul/03/dune-50-years-on-science-fiction-novel-world.

15. Dune Novels, accessed October 12, 2023, https://dunenovels.com/.

16. Adam Roberts, *The History of Science Fiction* (New York: Palgrave Macmillan, 2006), 234.

17. In the original publication, the "Terminology" is in the front of the book. In subsequent paperback versions, it is placed near the end. References here are from the first edition published by Chilton Books in 1965.

18. First mentioned in "Terminology of the Imperium," xvii–xviii

19. Herbert, *Dune*, 278.

20. Bruce Sterling, Preface to *Burning Chrome*, by William Gibson (New York: HarperCollins, 1986), xiv.

21. Sara R. Horowitz, "Marge Piercy," Shalvi/Hyman Encyclopedia of Jewish Women, June 23, 2021, https://jwa.org/encyclopedia/article/piercy-marge.

22. Jay Michaelson, "Golem: Making Men of Clay: Can Imitating God Extend to the Creative Realm?" My Jewish Learning, accessed October 12, 2023, https://www.myjewishlearning.com/article/golem/.

23. Piercy, *He, She, and It: A Novel*, 78.

24. Marge Piercy, *He, She, and It: A Novel* (New York: Knopf, 1991), 37.

25. Thomas M. Disch, *The Dreams Our Stuff Is Made Of: How Science Fiction Conquered the World* (New York: Touchstone, 1998), 170.

26. David Seed, "The Strategic Defense Initiative: A Utopian Fantasy," in *Future Wars: The Anticipations and the Fears*, ed. David Seed (Liverpool, UK: Liverpool University Press, 2012), 184–85.

27. Disch, *Dreams*, 71.

28. Quoted in Roger Luckhurst, *Science Fiction* (Cambridge, UK: Polity, 2005), 201.

29. Further context on science fiction authors and the SDI, along with Spinrad's claim, are in Seed, "Strategic Defense Initiative," 182.

30. Javier Sethness, "Toward and Ecologically Based Post-Capitalism: Interview with Novelist Kim Stanley Robinson," Truthout, March 17, 2018, https://truthout.org/articles/toward-an-ecologically-based-post-capitalism-interview-with-novelist-kim-stanley-robinson/.

31. See Nate Hagens (director of the Institute for the Study of Energy and Our Future), "Kim Stanley Robinson: 'Climate, Fiction, and the Future': The Great Simplification #66," video, 1:23:30, April 12, 2023, https://www.youtube.com/watch?v=Xc53KPv7flk&t=1280s.

32. Kim Stanley Robinson, *New York 2140* (New York: Orbit, 2017).

33. Jake Swearingen, "Kim Stanley Robinson's *New York 2140*: To Save the City, We Had to Drown It," *New York Magazine*, March 27, 2017, https://nymag.com/intelligencer/2017/03/kim-stanley-robinsons-new-york-2140-review-a-drowned-nyc.html.

34. Kim Stanley Robinson, *The Ministry for the Future* (New York: Orbit, 2020).

35. As late as the 1920s, the question of whether zeppelins or airplanes were the future was still, pardon the pun, up in the air. See Alexander Rose, *Empires of the Sky: Zeppelins, Airplanes, and Two Men's Epic Duel to Rule the World* (New York: Random House, 2020).

36. Kim Stanley Robinson, "Empty Half the Earth of Its Humans. It's the Only Way to Save the Planet," *Guardian*, March 20, 2018, https://www.theguardian.com/cities/2018/mar/20/save-the-planet-half-earth-kim-stanley-robinson.

37. Robinson, "Empty Half the Earth."

38. In this case, Wikipedia is acceptable, so see Wikipedia, "Cyberpunk," updated October 7, 2023, https://en.wikipedia.org/wiki/Cyberpunk.

39. Robinson, "Empty Half the Earth."

SUGGESTED READING

Evans, Rebecca. "New Wave Science Fiction and the Dawn of the Environmental Movement." In *The Cambridge History of Science Fiction*, edited by Gerry Caravan and Eric Carl Link, 436–37. New York: Cambridge University Press, 2019.

Horowitz, Sara R. "Marge Piercy." Shalvi/Hyman Encyclopedia of Jewish Women. June 23, 2021. https://jwa.org/encyclopedia/article/piercy-marge.

Lear, Linda. *Rachel Carson: Witness for Nature*. New York: Henry Holt, 1997.

Roberts, Adam. *The History of Science Fiction*. New York: Palgrave Macmillan, 2006.

Robinson, Kim Stanley. "Empty Half the Earth of Its Humans. It's the Only Way to Save the Planet." *Guardian*, March 20, 2018. https://www.theguardian.com/cities/2018/mar/20/save-the-planet-half-earth-kim-stanley-robinson.

Chapter 8

Confronting the Color Line

Afrofuturism, Science Fiction, and Dissent

This chapter considers how Afrofuturism can be integrated into the study of African American and US history or serve as a mechanism for dissent by a minority group.
    Classes this lesson can be used for:

- US history
- African American history
- Introduction to liberal arts

Science fiction films and texts:

- P. Djèlí Clark, *The Black God's Drums* (New York: Tom Doherty, 2018)
- W. E. Burghardt Du Bois, "The Comet," in *Darkwater: Voices from within the Veil* (New York: Harcourt, Brace and Howe, 1920)
- *The World, the Flesh, and the Devil*, directed by Ranald MacDougall, written by M. P. Shiel, Ferdinand Reyher, and Ranald MacDougall (MGM, 1959)

At first glance, *The World, the Flesh, and the Devil* seems a typical example of the postapocalyptic films produced during the early Cold War.[1] The film begins with mining engineer Ralph (played by Harry Belafonte) inspecting a mine in Pennsylvania when he is trapped by a cave-in. After a few days, the sounds of rescuers digging toward him ceases, and he must find a way out himself. On emerging from the mine, he discovers the world empty of people. Over the course of the next few scenes, it is revealed that an unnamed country has spread radioactive isotopes across the globe, killing most of the world's population.

Ralph wanders an empty New York City for days, and eventually the loneliness drives him to the edge of madness. Before his mental state disintegrates completely, he meets another survivor, a women named Sarah (played by Inger Stevens). Ralph and Sarah develop a close relationship verging on sexual intimacy, which Ralph seems reluctant to consummate. Another survivor, Benson (Mel Ferrer) arrives by boat, and his presence creates a love triangle that leads to the two men trying to kill each other for possession of the last woman in the world. In the end, peace is established between the alpha males; all three walk off holding hands as the credits read, "The Beginning."

The last-man-in-the-world theme in science fiction predates the Cold War, as does the notion that some natural or man-made disaster could wipe out humankind.[2] The imagery of an empty New York City has also been used in a variety of postapocalyptic movies over the past century; the 2007 version of *I Am Legend* is perhaps the most notable recent example.[3] What makes *The World, the Flesh, and the Devil* fascinating for the student of history is the racial context of the film. Ralph is an African American—and it is important to remember that the United States was still a highly segregated society in 1959. As for the other survivors, Sarah is White, and Benson is Latin in appearance.

Despite the ethnic diversity of the characters, racist comments play no overt role in the film's dialogue. While Ralph and Sarah do not develop an explicit romantic relationship prior to Benson's arrival, it can be assumed that the preapocalyptic color barrier might play a role in his hesitation to engage in intimacy. It is also likely that the Hollywood studio was unwilling to go so far as to show an interracial kiss in 1959. When tension erupts between the two men over the last woman on Earth, it is Benson, the White man, who initiates the violence, and it is Ralph who deescalates the situation and puts down his weapon. Finally, it is Sarah who serves as the mediator between the two men, providing the harmony for the ending scene.

The *New York Times* film reviewer was not impressed with the film and argued, "Social distinctions and mating are considered in the most conventional terms, and a potentially fascinating contemplation of a unique sociological change is discarded in favor of a cliché: two men and a girl on a desert isle." Indeed, he accused Hollywood of being "cautious" about the issue of race.[4] Others might disagree; after all, it was the casting rather than the original storyline that introduced the theme of race.[5] It is also a proof text that science fiction is a genre that pushes boundaries and challenges conventional assumptions, even at the end of the world.

Interestingly, the producers of *The World, the Flesh, and the Devil* credit M. P. Shiel's novel *The Purple Cloud* as one of the sources for the script.[6] Shiel's story is part of the last-man genre, where the protagonist survives an unexplained global catastrophe, eventually is driven mad by loneliness, finally finds another survivor (a woman, of course), and by the end of the story implicitly emerges as Adam to the other survivor's Eve. The book, which remains in print, is like many science fiction stories of the early twentieth century in that the protagonist is White.[7]

Although the writers, director, and producers of *The World* claimed they were drawing upon Shiel's story, another short story entitled "The Comet," follows a plotline very similar to the 1959 film, including the racial dimension.[8] "The Comet" is an early example of Afrofuturism, and the author of the short story is civil rights activist W. E. B. Du Bois.[9]

The science fiction subgenre known as Afrofuturism has its origins in the nineteenth century, and in its earliest manifestations, it is "speculative fiction that treats African-American themes and addresses African-American concerns in the context of twentieth-century techno culture."[10] It is not surprising that African Americans are found among the earliest writers of science fiction, for the genre provides a venue for dissenting from dominant social and intellectual currents. In addition, science fiction tends to be segregated as a literary form, and in a highly segregated society, such as the mid-twentieth-century United States, the association would seem natural. Afrofuturists were like other science fiction writers in that they use the future, another planet, or the apocalypse as a mechanism to criticize contemporary society or promote radical ideas.[11]

Afrofuturism applies many of the same themes of early science fiction. For example, Edward Bellamy's famous *Looking Backward* describes a man transported a century into the future who finds that the United States has been transformed into a socialist utopia.[12] The novel then proceeds as a history lesson for the sleeper about how that transformation occurred. An example of a similar Afrofuturist story is Edward A. Johnson's *Light Ahead for the Negro*.[13] This novel follows a format similar to Bellamy's, albeit focused on racial issues. In this version, an idealistic White man comes out of suspended animation a century in the future and learns about the progress that African Americans have made in education, the sciences, and medicine. Not a socialist utopia, per Bellamy, but an argument that gradual change in race relations is possible.[14]

Du Bois's "The Comet" follows an apocalyptic storyline comparable to Shiel's, but the setting is limited to the island of Manhattan. Jim is an African American messenger who works at a White-owned bank. He is in the basement vault when a passing comet releases a poison gas that kills everyone in the city and perhaps the world. Wandering through the city, Jim meditates on his changed circumstances as he walks into the ruins of a restaurant that would not have served him the day before. Now, thanks to the apocalypse, that Jim Crow world is destroyed. He then comes across Julia, a White woman survivor. Believing that they are the only two people left in the world, the two confront their past racial assumptions and contemplate how they may be responsible for the rebirth of humanity. As I have shown, the Adam-and-Eve motif is common in these last-man tales.[15]

Before the two consummate their union, Julia's fiancé, father, and a rescue party arrive. It seems the destruction from the poison gas was limited only to Manhattan. The transformation in Julia's attitude toward Jim is immediate; explaining to her fiancé what happened to her over the past few days and how Jim saved her, she also stops looking directly at the Black man. Angered that a Black man was in such close physical proximity to a White woman, the White men consider lynching Jim. It seems the old racial hierarchy is easily restored once the apocalypse is over. Julia does defend Jim, asserting that he did nothing wrong (i.e., he did not touch her); after receiving a cash reward from Julia's father, Jim walks a gauntlet of men who still consider lynching him. At the end of the story, Jim is reunited with an unnamed woman, perhaps his wife.[16]

Afrofuturism evolved in the twentieth century, just as the wider science fiction genre did. While many mainstream writers continued to avoid discussions of race, slavery, or segregation, examples of literary confrontation with these issues can also be found if you look in the right place. Interestingly, one of the earliest popular culture media to confront racism directly was Marvel Comics' *Fantastic Four*, where the character of the Black Panther is first introduced in issue 52.[17] T'challa, the ruler of the fictional country of Wakanda, is very likely the first Black superhero in American comics.[18] While still a child, T'challa defends his kingdom after his father is murdered by modern-day imperialists after the precious mineral vibranium. After assuming the throne, T'challa sells small amounts of vibranium, which is only found in Wakanda, to bring his people out of poverty. He adopts the Black Panther guise as a means of protecting his nation from outside predators.

In addition to creating a strong and likeable Black character, a later issue of *Fantastic Four* confronts the system of apartheid.[19] Two members of the Fantastic Four, the Thing and Human Torch, are told that T'challa was tracking stolen vibranium and has gone missing. It turns out that he is a prisoner in the racist republic of Rudyarda, a not-so-subtle play on the name of the former poet laureate of the empire Rudyard Kipling. Rudyarda is also a not-so-subtle substitute for the Republic of South Africa, where the population is segregated into two groups in public places: "Coloreds" and "Europeans." The Thing and the Human Torch wonder about a people who insist on maintaining such distinctions despite having lived in Africa for several generations.

After rescuing T'challa, the Thing demolishes an exit gate, physically and symbolically destroying the artificial distinction between people. "I didn't do it for you," the Thing tells T'challa. "I did it for me." As a being whose physical characteristics are often described as grotesque, Ben Grimm (the Thing) knows a few things about discrimination. Interestingly, in 2002, it was revealed that Jack Kirby, one of the creators of the *Fantastic Four* franchise, intended Grimm's character to be identified as a Jew.[20]

By the 1970s, a cadre of African American writers were challenging accepted notions of race and ethnicity in science fiction. Many of these authors also integrated other movements into the genre, such as the new wave, alternate history, and steampunk, into their work. P. Djèlí Clark's *The Black God's Drums* is an alternate history-novel, with elements of steampunk, that is a good book for classroom use.[21] As discussed in chapter 4, alternate history often serves a political agenda.

One of the most popular scenarios in alternate history is the Confederacy either winning the American Civil War or at least not losing it. For devotees of the Lost Cause, the South winning the war is a fantasy scenario in which the future would have been better, at least for the White population, had the Southern way of life continued.[22] The nightmare scenario of a Confederate victory usually describes the creation of a more violent, even genocidal, society in the American South.[23] Simply put, in the nightmare scenario, the world would not have been better had the outcome been different.

Clark's *Black God's Drums* fits best into the nightmare scenario although from an Afrofuturism point of view; that is to say, it incorporates Afro-Caribbean mysticism and gods as players in a plotline focused on Black characters. In addition to having some of the narrative written in Afro-Caribbean dialect, it features common steampunk elements, such as zeppelin-style airships. Set in New Orleans years after the Confederacy fought the Union to a standstill, the novel focuses on Creeper, a street child who has a special rapport with one of the gods. In addition to parts of the American South, the action also takes the reader to Haiti, where Creeper helps thwart a conspiracy of Confederate soldiers trying to obtain godlike power.

Early Afrofuturism employs science fiction stories to address the African American experience. By the early twenty-first century, the movement had expanded its focus to include the intersection of the African diaspora with science, technology, and philosophy. For example, N. K. Jemisin is a contemporary writer who has expanded the boundaries of old Afrofuturism and incorporates many attributes of contemporary science fiction to create a unique style in her novels.[24] She won the Hugo Award three years in a row (2015–2017), an unprecedented event.[25] Jemisin is among a cadre of talented writers who have pushed science fiction to new levels of engagement with politics, racism, and other issues of contemporary concern.

Interestingly, if not surprisingly, there was a conservative pushback on the developing prominence of such writers as Jemisin. A right-wing movement called the Sad Puppies, comprised of a handful of science fiction writers and some fans, felt the Hugo Awards were captive to political correctness and were overemphasizing the accomplishments of minority writers, at the expense of more traditional science fiction stories and authors.[26] Allying with the Rabid Puppies, the Sad Puppies tried to flood the Hugo nominations with what they considered more traditional topics and writers. The movement lasted for only a few years (2013–2017), and its impact on the award was neither direct nor long-lasting.[27]

CLASS QUESTIONS AND EXERCISES

1. Could Du Bois's "The Comet" have served as one of the inspirations for *The World, the Flesh, and the Devil*?
2. Why might Hollywood have been reluctant to cite an African American author as a source in 1959? Or was the last-man theme so well ingrained in popular culture that enough source material could be found without knowing about "The Comet"?
3. What role does popular culture play in bringing controversial ideas to the public?
4. How does the Black Panther story differ from stories about White-African interaction? You can use either the comic book stories or the 2018 movie.[28]
5. Research the science fiction authors who led the Sad Puppies' campaign. Are their science fiction stories examples of more traditional writing?
6. Are you able to identify where Afrofuturist writers are located on the political spectrum?

NOTES

1. *The World, the Flesh, and the Devil*, dir. Ranald MacDougall, writ. M. P. Shiel, Ferdinand Reyher, and Ranald MacDougall (MGM, 1959). Among a small sample of the notable (not necessarily good) films of the era are *Day the World Ended*, dir. Roger Corman, writ. Lou Rusoff (ARC, 1955); and *Five*, dir. Arch Oboler, writ. Arch Oboler and James Weldon Johnson (Columbia Pictures, 1951).

2. For a survey of the last-man-on-Earth literature, see Amy J. Ransom, "The First Last Man: Cousin de Grainville's Le Dernier homme," Science Fiction Studies 41, no. 2 (July 2014): 314–40.

3. *I Am Legend*, dir. Francis Lawrence, writ. Mark Protosevich, Akiva Goldsman, and Richard Matheson (Warner Bros., 2007). Interestingly, Richard Matheson, *I Am Legend* (New York: Fawcett, 1954), was adapted into *The Omega Man*, dir. Boris Sagal, writ. John William Corrington, Joyce Hooper Corrington, and Richard Matheson (Warner Bros., 1971), which pairs a White actor (Charlton Heston) with an African American actress (Rosalind Cash).

4. Bosley Crowther, "Screen: Radioactive City; 'The World, the Flesh and the Devil' Opens," *New York Times*, May 21, 1959, https://www.nytimes.com/1959/05/21/archives/screen-radioactive-city-the-world-the-flesh-and-the-devil-opens.html.

5. See Tracy A. Dennis-Tlwary, "Why Science Fiction Speaks the Language of Anxiety," Psychology Today, March 1, 2022, https://www.psychologytoday.com/us/blog/more-feeling/202203/why-science-fiction-speaks-the-language-anxiety.

6. M. P. Shiel, *The Purple Cloud* (London: Chatto and Windus, 1901).

7. For context on M. P. Shiel, see Terry Harpold, "European Science Fiction in the Nineteenth Century," in *The Cambridge History of Science Fiction*, edited by Gerry Canavan and Eric Carl Link, 50–68 (New York: Cambridge University Press, 2019), 66–67.

8. W. E. Burghardt Du Bois, "The Comet," in *Darkwater: Voices from within the Veil* (New York: Harcourt, Brace and Howe, 1920).

9. W. Andrew Shephard, "Afrofuturism in the Nineteenth and Twentieth Centuries," in *The Cambridge History of Science Fiction*, edited by Gerry Canavan and Eric Carl Link, 101–19 (New York: Cambridge University Press, 2019), 117.

10. Quoted in Shephard, "Afrofuturism," 101.

11. Shephard, "Afrofuturism," 102–3.

12. Edward Bellamy, *Looking Backward, 2000–1887* (Boston: Ticknor, 1888).

13. E. A. Johnson, *Light Ahead for the Negro* (New York: Grafton Press, 1904).

14. Shephard, "Afrofuturism," 104.

15. Shephard, "Afrofuturism," 110.

16. W. E. B. Du Bois, "The Comet," in *Darkwater: Voices from within the Veil* (New York: Harcourt, Brace and Howe, 1920), http://zacharyrawe.com/sem_6_the_comet_dubois.pdf, 61. For the full volume that the short story appears in, see Internet Archive, https://archive.org/details/darkwatervoicesf00duborich/page/n11/mode/2up.

17. Stan Lee, *Fantastic Four*, no. 52 (July 1966).

18. National Museum of American History, "Black Panther, Vol. 1 No. 4," Smithsonian, accessed October 12, 2023, https://www.si.edu/object/black-panther-vol-1-no-4%3Anmah_1894264.

19. Stan Lee, *Fantastic Four*, no. 119 (February 1972).

20. Andrew Alan Smith, "Jack Kirby: The Not-So-Secret Identity of the Thing," in *Working-Class Comic Book Heroes: Class Conflict and Populist Politics in Comics*, ed. Marc DiPaolo, 195–201 (University of Mississippi Press, 2018).

21. P. Djèlí Clark, *The Black God's Drums* (New York: Tom Doherty, 2018). For biographical information, see P. Djèlí Clark, "About," 2022, https://pdjeliclark.com/about/.

22. See Gavriel D. Rosenfeld, "Why Do We Ask 'What If?' Reflections on the Function of Alternate History," *History and Theory*, theme issue 41 (December 2002): 90–103, for discussion of fantasy and nightmare scenarios.

23. An example of this approach is Harry Turtledove's Southern Victory series. Wikipedia, "*Southern Victory*," updated July 18, 2023, https://en.wikipedia.org/wiki/Southern_Victory.

24. I owe this information to my colleague Professor Cassie Fetters, an expert on African American literature who teaches Jemisin's work in her classes.

25. N. K. Jemisin, *The Fifth Season* (New York: Orbit, 2015); N. K. Jemisin, *The Obelisk Gate* (New York: Orbit, 2016); and N. K. Jemisin, *The Stone Sky* (New York: Orbit, 2017).

26. See Wikipedia, "Sad Puppies," updated July 12, 2023, https://en.wikipedia.org/wiki/Sad_Puppies.

27. See Michael Schaub, "'Sad Puppies' Campaign Fails to Undermine Sci-Fi Diversity at the Hugo Awards," *Los Angeles Times*, August 24, 2015, https://www.latimes.com/books/jacketcopy/la-et-jc-no-love-for-sad-puppies-hugo-awards-20150824-story.html. Science fiction author John Scalzi also discusses the Sad Puppies in his blog, *Whatever: Furiously Reasonable*, accessed October 12, 2023, https://whatever.scalzi.com/.

28. *Black Panther*, dir. Ryan Coogler, writ. Ryan Coogler, Joe Robert Cole, and Stan Lee (Marvel Studios, 2018).

SUGGESTED READINGS

DiPaolo, Marc, ed. *Working-Class Comic Book Heroes: Class Conflict and Populist Politics in Comics* Jackson: University of Mississippi Press, 2018.

Harpold, Terry. "European Science Fiction in the Nineteenth Century." In *The Cambridge History of Science Fiction*, edited by Gerry Canavan and Eric Carl Link, 50–68. New York: Cambridge University Press, 2019.

Shephard, W. Andrew. "Afrofuturism in the Nineteenth and Twentieth Centuries." In *The Cambridge History of Science Fiction*, edited by Gerry Canavan and Eric Carl Link, 101–19. New York: Cambridge University Press, 2019.

Conclusion
A Brief How-To Guide

Using science fiction as a primary source opens new vistas for history students. As I detail in previous chapters, the not-so-secret ingredient of science fiction (SF) is history, and as Samuel Delany once asserted, "SF is not about the future. SF is in dialogue with the present. It works by setting up a dialogue with the here-and-now, a dialogue as rich and intricate as the writer can make it."[1] Thus, properly evaluated, a science fiction text or film can be a valuable primary source, for it reveals the anxieties, hopes, and aspirations of an era.[2]

In his classic novel *1984*, George Orwell argues, "Who controls the past controls the future: who controls the present controls the past."[3] Conversely, when science fiction writers create a future, they often use it to critique the present. A prime example of this is Margaret Atwood's novel *The Handmaid's Tale*; set at an indeterminant point in the future, Atwood criticizes both our contemporary failure to deal with environmental issues and the rising tide of religious fundamentalism that threatens women's rights.[4] Thus by crafting a "history of the future," she is trying to influence the present.

As the previous chapters show, a similar approach should be applied when evaluating work in the alternate-history genre. Whether it be a steampunk story with zeppelins crisscrossing the sky or a simple divergence in the historical record (e.g., the Confederacy wins the Battle of Gettysburg), how an author rewrites the past is almost certainly a political statement. In a sense, most historians practice a form of alternate history whenever we ask a class to consider a scenario distinct from what happened. Most teachers have at one point posited, "Suppose this happened instead of this."

FROM THE MACRO TO THE MICRO AND VICE VERSA

As an instructor, suppose you decide that using a science fiction text or film would be beneficial to your class; however, you did not necessarily find something in this book that fits your needs or interests. How, then, might you go about finding a source and crafting a lesson around it? There are two ways to approach developing a class module: from above and from below.

Let's consider the decision-making process from above. Suppose the class is a survey-level class of modern European history, and you want students to understand the intellectual tumult of the interwar years (1919–1939). As with any class preparation, you would likely start with a general survey of the period to familiarize yourself with the subject. For example, from John W. Boyer's *Austria: A History*, the instructor would discover that, as early as the eighteenth century, the Czech language was experiencing a renaissance. Indeed, language was a "constituent part of the culture of the Czech nation" and provided a core of the later development of nationalism and the vibrant literary landscape of the new nation.[5]

From the general textbook, you could then move to a specialized study of early-twentieth-century Czech culture; Thomas Ort's *Art and Life in Modernist Prague* details how science fiction literature was shaped by late Habsburg culture and then the Great War. Ort challenges the traditional image of the early twentieth century as a period of gloom among Central European intellectuals, pointing to their use of such literary tools as satire to critique modern society.[6] For more specific information on the history of science fiction, you could consult chapter 8 of Adam Roberts's *History of Science Fiction*.[7]

In your research, you discover the work of Karel Čapek (1890–1938), a Czech writer who introduced the word *robot* into the science fiction lexicon via his 1920 book *R.U.R.* (*Rossum's Universal Robots*).[8] Čapek is the author of *The Absolute at Large*, available in an inexpensive paperback edition from the University of Nebraska Press, which is a critique of capitalism, Marxism, and religious beliefs.[9] The Absolute is a machine that annihilates matter and produces cheap energy, which does two things: It enables the manufacture of consumer goods almost cost free, and it unleashes a religious mania among the population.

So the decision-making process works this way:

1. Decide which class to use a science fiction text or film.
2. Conduct a contextual reading on the intellectual, political, and literary history of the times.
3. Narrow down the subject matter (in this case, author Karol Čapek) that you would like the students to study.
4. Consider the availability of the source material. The easier it is to obtain, the better.
5. Present the students with a contextual lecture on the political and cultural history of post–World War I Central Europe, including biographical information on Karel Čapek.

Here is a sample assignment. After reading Čapek's *Absolute at Large*, answer the following questions:

1. In the *Absolute at Large*, identify the causes of the economic collapse and the Great War that followed. What was the Absolute, and what role did it play in creating the conflict?
2. Was Čapek's science fiction story intended to promote new scientific and political ideas?

Finding a text or film to use in class can also be done from the bottom up. Suppose a friend recommends you read Colson Whitehead's *Underground Railroad*, an alternate history of the Antebellum United States (c. 1850).[10] In this reality, the Underground Railroad is an actual subterranean train that helps escaped slaves travel northward, and the storyline follows characters through an American landscape that is an amalgamation of multiple eras.

Perhaps you know a great deal about American history but have little experience in using science fiction in the classroom. To develop an appropriate pedagogy, you could start by reading Gavriel Rosenfeld's "Why Do We Ask 'What If?'" on alternate history. Rosenfeld asserts that most alternate-history stories fit into either a fantasy or a nightmare scenario, and both serve a political agenda.[11] Do these typologies help explain Whitehead's novel? Furthermore, assigning the novel might be a good opportunity to introduce students to the concept of Afrofuturism and discuss whether *The Underground Railroad* is an example of the genre.[12]

As a teacher of American history, you might find it interesting how Whitehead draws on contemporary narratives written by men who escaped slavery, such as Frederick Douglass. Does his use of the female protagonist Cora reflect our contemporary desires to provide a more gendered approach to our historical understanding? Whitehead also uses issues from other eras of US history, such as the Tuskegee syphilis experiments and the eugenicists' campaign to sterilize undesirables, as plot devices. What does this tell us about the author's political ideology?

So, the decision-making process might work as follows:

1. You find an interesting science fiction book: in this case, Colson Whitehead's *The Underground Railroad*. Where does the story diverge from actual historical events?
2. You establish a pedagogical approach for your lesson plan. For example, how does alternate history promote a specific political point of view?
3. It is important to recognize that this novel is *not* a document from Antebellum America but of early-twenty-first-century America.

Therefore, the contextual lecture for the students is on contemporary politics and culture.

Some potential discussion questions:

1. Is Whitehead's novel an example of a nightmare scenario or a fantasy scenario?
2. What political ideology does it advocate?
3. Is the novel an example of Afrofuturism?

Similar approaches can be done with Russian, German, British, and Anglophone science fiction, as long as you remember that the genre is a tool for teaching. Richard Stites's observation about Russian science fiction applies to the genre across national boundaries and times: "[T]he world of fantasy, like the world of myth and legend, reveals and evokes deep layers, archaic dreams and longings that better describe feelings and anxieties than some conventional acts of political adherence."[13] Our job as students of history is to peel back those layers and develop a more nuanced view of the past. Perhaps counterintuitively, studying stories set in the future can help us understand the past better.

NOTES

1. Quoted in Gary K. Wolfe, *The Known and the Unknown: The Iconography of Science Fiction* (Kent, OH: Kent State University Press, 1979), 18.
2. Tracy A. Dennis-Tlwary, "Why Science Fiction Speaks the Language of Anxiety," *Psychology Today*, March 1, 2022, https://www.psychologytoday.com/us/blog/more-feeling/202203/why-science-fiction-speaks-the-language-anxiety.
3. George Orwell, *1984: A Novel* (New York: New American Library, 1977), 44.
4. Margaret Atwood, *The Handmaid's Tale* (Toronto: McClelland and Stewart, 1985).
5. John W. Boyer, *Austria, 1867–1955* (Oxford, UK: Oxford University Press, 2022), 15.
6. Thomas Ort, *Art and Life in Modernist Prague: Karol Čapek and His Generation, 1911–1938* (New York: Palgrave Macmillan, 2013).
7. Adam Roberts, "The Early Twentieth Century: High Modernist Science Fiction," in *The History of Science Fiction* (New York: Palgrave Macmillan, 2005).
8. Karel Čapek, *R.U.R. (Rossum's Universal Robots)*, trans. Paul Selver and Nigel Playfair (Mineola, NY: Dover, 2001).
9. Karel Čapek, *The Absolute at Large* (1922; Lincoln: University of Nebraska Press, 2005).

10. Colson Whitehead, *The Underground Railroad: A Novel* (New York: Doubleday, 2016).

11. Gavriel D. Rosenfeld "Why Do We Ask 'What If?' Reflections on the Function of Alternate History," *History and Theory*, theme issue 41 (December 2002): 90–103.

12. See W. Andrew Shephard, "Afrofuturism in the Nineteenth and Twentieth Centuries," in *The Cambridge History of Science Fiction*, ed. Gerry Canavan and Eric Carl Link, 101–19 (New York: Cambridge University Press, 2019).

13. Richard Stites, *Revolutionary Dreams: Utopian Vision and Experimental Life in the Russian Revolution* (New York: Oxford University Press, 1989), 34.

Bibliography

PRIMARY SOURCES

Books and Short Stories
Atwood, Margaret. *The Handmaid's Tale*. Toronto: McClelland and Stewart, 1985.
Baxter, Stephen. *The Massacre of Mankind: The Sequel to* The War of the Worlds. New York: Crown, 2017.
Bellamy, Edward. *Looking Backward, 2000–1887*. Boston: Ticknor, 1888.
Čapek, Karel. *The Absolute At Large*. 1922; Lincoln: University of Nebraska Press, 2005.
———. *R.U.R. (Rossum's Universal Robots)*. Translated by Paul Selver and Nigel Playfair. Mineola, NY: Dover, 2001.
Carson, Rachel. *Silent Spring*. Boston: Houghton Mifflin, 1962.
Clark, P. Djèlí. *The Black God's Drums*. New York: Tom Doherty, 2018.
Dick, Philip K. *The Man in the High Castle: A Novel*. New York: Putnam, 1962.
Du Bois, W. E. Burghardt. "The Comet." In *Darkwater: Voices from within the Veil*. New York: Harcourt, Brace and Howe, 1920. http://zacharyrawe.com/sem_6_the_comet_dubois.pdf.
Finney, Jack. *The Body Snatchers*. New York: Dell, 1955.
Gernsback, Hugo. "Will the Germans Bomb New York?" *Electrical Experimenter* 6, no. 3 (July 1918): 156–57, 192.
Haldeman, Joe. *The Forever War*. New York: St. Martin's Press, 1974.
Harris, Richard. *Fatherland*. New York: Random House, 2006.
Heinlein, Robert A. *Farmer in the Sky*. New York: Scribner, 1950.
———. *Starship Troopers*. New York: Putnam, 1959.
Herbert, Frank. *Dune*. Philadelphia: Chilton Books, 1965.
Jemisin, N. K. *The Fifth Season*. New York: Orbit, 2015.
———. *The Obelisk Gate*. New York: Orbit, 2016.
———. *The Stone Sky*. New York: Orbit, 2017.
Johnson, E. A. *Light Ahead for the Negro*. New York: Grafton Press, 1904.
Kornbluth, Cyril M. "Two Dooms." Venture Science Fiction 2, no. 4 (July 1958): 4–49.
Lee, Stan. *Fantastic Four*, no. 52 (July 1966).
———. *Fantastic Four*, no. 119 (February 1972).

Lewis, Sinclair. *It Can't Happen Here: A Novel*. Garden City, NY: Doubleday, Doran, 1935.

MacLeod, Ian R. "The Summer Isles." *Asimov's Science Fiction* 22, nos. 10/11 (October/November 1998): 172–226.

Matheson, Richard. *I Am Legend*. New York: Fawcett, 1954.

Mueller, Richard. "Jew If by Sea." *Fantasy and Science Fiction Magazine* (May 2004).

Nowlan, Philip Francis. "The Airlords of Han." *Amazing Stories* 3, no. 12 (March 1929): 1106–36.

———. "Armageddon—2419 A.D." *Amazing Stories* 3, no. 5 (August 1928): 422–49.

———. *Armageddon 2419 AD*. New York: Ace Books, 1962.

Orwell, George. *1984: A Novel*. New York: New American Library, 1977.

———. *Animal Farm: A Fairy Story*. London: Secker and Warburg, 1945.

Piercy, Marge. *He, She, and It: A Novel*. New York: Knopf, 1991.

Robinson, Kim Stanley. *The Ministry for the Future*. New York: Orbit, 2020.

———. *New York 2140*. New York: Orbit, 2017.

Schachner, Nat. "Ancestral Voices." *Astounding Stories* 12, no. 4 (December 1933): 70–82.

Serviss, Garret P. *Edison's Conquest of Mars*. 1898; Los Angeles: Carcosa House, 1947.

Verne, Jules. *The Begum's Millions*. 1879; Middletown, CT: Wesleyan University Press, 2005.

———. *Invasion of the Sea*. 1905; Middletown, CT: Wesleyan University Press, 2001.

"War of the Worlds by H. G. Wells." *Classics Illustrated*, no. 124 (January 1955). https://archive.org/details/WarOfTheWorldsClassic1955.

Wells, H. G. "The Land Ironclads." *Strand Magazine* (December 1903): 501–2.

———. *The War in the Air*. Bison Frontiers of Imagination. 1908; Lincoln: University of Nebraska Press, 2002.

———. *The War of the Worlds*. New York: Harper and Brothers, 1898.

Whitehead, Colson. *The Underground Railroad: A Novel*. New York: Doubleday, 2016.

Wright, Sydney Fowler. *Deluge*. London: F. Wright, 1927.

———. *Deluge*. Edited by Brian Stableford. Middletown, CT: Wesleyan University Press, 2003.

Wyndham, John. *The Chrysalids*. 1955; New York: New York Review Books, 2008.

Films and Television Shows

Black Panther. Directed by Ryan Coogler. Written by Ryan Coogler, Joe Robert Cole, and Stan Lee. Marvel Studios, 2018.

Day the World Ended. Directed by Roger Corman. Written by Lou Rusoff. ARC, 1955.

Deluge. Directed by Felix E. Feist. Written by S. Fowler Wright, John F. Goodrich, and Warren Duff. RKO, 1933. https://www.youtube.com/watch?v=CnUVWmtaqHE.

Dune: Part One. Directed by Denis Villeneuve. Written by Jon Spaihts, Denis Villeneuve, and Eric Roth. Warner Bros., 2021.

Dune: Part Two. Directed by Denis Villeneuve. Written by Denis Villeneuve, Jon Spaihts, and Frank Herbert. Warner Bros., 2024.

Fatherland. Directed by Christopher Menaul. Written by Robert Harris, Stanley Weiser, and Ron Hutchinson. HBO Pictures, 1994.

Five. Directed by Arch Oboler. Written by Arch Oboler and James Weldon Johnson. Columbia Pictures, 1951.
Five Million Years to Earth. Directed by Roy Ward Baker. Written by Nigel Kneale. Hammer Films, 1967. https://archive.org/details/quatermassandthepit_202002.
I Am Legend. Directed by Francis Lawrence. Written by Mark Protosevich, Akiva Goldsman, and Richard Matheson. Warner Bros., 2007.
Man in the High Castle. Created by Frank Spotnitz. Aired 2015–2019 on Amazon Prime Video.
The Omega Man. Directed by Boris Sagal. Written by John William Corrington, Joyce Hooper Corrington, and Richard Matheson. Warner Bros., 1971.
Planet of the Apes. Directed by Franklin J. Schaffner. Written by Michael Wilson, Rod Serling, and Pierre Boulle. Twentieth Century Fox, 1968.
"Planet of the Apes (5/5) Movie Clip—Statue of Liberty (1968) HD." Video, 2:42. August 17, 2015. https://www.youtube.com/watch?v=mDLS12_a-fk.
Them! Directed by Gordon Douglas. Written by Ted Sherdeman, Russell S. Hughes, and George Worthing Yates. Warner Bros., 1954.
Things to Come. Directed by William Cameron Menzies. Written by H. G. Wells. London Films, 1936.
Twilight Zone. Season 1, episode 22, "The Monsters are Due on Maple Street." Directed by Ron Winston. Written by Rod Serling. Aired March 4, 1960, on CBS.
Twilight Zone. Season 3, episode 9, "Deaths-Head Revisited." Directed by Don Medford. Written by Rod Serling. Aired November 10, 1961, on CBS.
Twilight Zone. Season 4, episode 4, "He's Alive." Directed by Stuart Rosenberg. Written by Rod Serling. Aired January 24, 1963, on CBS.
The World, the Flesh, and the Devil. Directed by Ranald MacDougall. Written by M. P. Shiel, Ferdinand Reyher, and Ranald MacDougall. MGM, 1959.

SECONDARY SOURCES

Abbott, Carl. *Frontiers Past and Future: Science Fiction and the American West*. Lawrence: University Press of Kansas, 2006.
Adrian, Jack. "Nigel Kneale: Creator of Quatermass." *Independent*, November 2, 2006. http://news.independent.co.uk/people/obituaries/article1948184.ece.
Aldiss, Brian W. "Harris, John Wyndham Parkes Lucas Beynon [*pseud*. John Wyndham] (1903–1969)." *Oxford Dictionary of National Biography*. January 8, 2015. https://doi.org/10.1093/ref:odnb/33728.
Ashley, Mike, and Robert A. W. Lowndes. *The Gernsback Days: A Study of the Evolution of Modern Science Fiction from 1911 to 1936*. Holicong, PA: Wildside Press, 2004.
Asimov, Isaac, ed. *Before the Golden Age: A Science Fiction Anthology of the 1930s*. Garden City, NY: Doubleday, 1974.
Bachrach, Fabian. "Hugo Gernsback Is Dead at 83; Author, Publisher and Inventor; 'Father of Modern Science Fiction' Predicted Radar—Beamed TV in '28 'One to Forsee for All.'" *New York Times*, August 20, 1967.

Baumann, Timo, and Daniel Marc Segesser. "Shadows of Total War in French and British Military Journals, 1918–1939." In *The Shadows of Total War: Europe, East Asia, and the United States, 1919–1939*, edited by Roger Chickering and Stig Förster, 197–222. New York: German Historical Institute and Cambridge University Press, 2003.

Best Sci Fi Books. "The Bestselling Science Fiction Books of All Time." November 28, 2021. https://best-sci-fi-books.com/the-bestselling-science-fiction-books-of-all-time/.

Bialer, Uri. *The Shadow of the Bomber: The Fear of Air Attack and British Politics*. London: Royal Historical Society, 1980.

Bleiler, Everett F. *Science Fiction: The Gernsback Years*. Kent, OH: Kent State University Press, 1998.

Bogdanov, Alexander. *Red Star: The First Bolshevik Utopia*. Edited by Loren R. Graham and Richard Stites. Translated by Charles Rougle. Bloomington: Indiana University Press, 1984.

Bowler, Peter J. *A History of the Future: Prophets of Progress from H. G. Wells to Isaac Asimov*. New York: Cambridge University Press, 2017.

Boyer, John W. *Austria, 1867–1955*. Oxford, UK: Oxford University Press, 2022.

Canavan, Gerry, and Eric Carl Link, eds. *The Cambridge History of Science Fiction*. New York: Cambridge University Press, 2019.

Carter, Paul A. "From 'Nat' to 'Nathan': The Liberal Arts Odyssey of a Pulpster." In *Styles of Creation: Aesthetic Techniques and the Creation of Fictional Worlds*, edited by George Slusser and Eric S. Rabkin, 58–78. Athens: University of Georgia Press, 1992.

———. "The Phantom Dictator: Science Fiction Discovers Hitler." in *The Creation of Tomorrow: Fifty Years of Magazine Science Fiction*. New York: Columbia University Press, 1977.

Chapman, James, and Nicholas Cull. *Projecting Tomorrow: Science Fiction and Popular Culture*. London: I. B. Taurus, 2013.

Cheng, John. *Astounding Wonder: Imagining Science and Science Fiction in Interwar America*. Philadelphia: University of Pennsylvania Press, 2012.

Clark, P. Djèlí. "About." 2022. https://pdjeliclark.com/about/.

Clarke, I. F., ed. *The Great War with Germany, 1890–1914: Fictions and Fantasies of the War-to-Come*. Liverpool, UK: Liverpool University Press, 1997.

———. *The Pattern of Expectation 1644–2001*. London: Jonathan Cape, 1979.

———. *Voices Prophesying War: Future Wars, 1763–3749*. Oxford, UK: Oxford University Press, 1992.

Clute, John, and Peter Nicholas. *The Encyclopedia of Science Fiction*. 3rd ed. London: Orbit, 1999.

Corcoran, Miranda. "Teaching History and Theory through Popular Culture: My First Time Designing a Module." US Studies Online. November 17, 2014. https://usso.uk/2014/11/17/teaching-history-and-theory-through-popular-culture-my-first-time-designing-a-module/.

Crossley, Robert. *Imagining Mars: A Literary History*. Middletown, CT: Wesleyan University Press, 2011.

Crowther, Bosley. "Screen: Radioactive City; 'The World, the Flesh and the Devil' Opens." *New York Times*, May 21, 1959. https://www.nytimes.com/1959/05/21/archives/screen-radioactive-city-the-world-the-flesh-and-the-devil-opens.html.

Csicsery-Ronay, Istvan, Jr. "Empire." In *The Routledge Companion to Science Fiction*, edited by Mark Bould, Andrew Butler, Adam Roberts, and Sherryl Vint, 365–66. New York: Routledge, 2009.

Cull, Nicholas. *Projecting Tomorrow: Science Fiction and Popular Culture*. London: I. B. Taurus, 2013.

———. "Reading, Viewing, and Tuning in to the Cold War." In *The Cambridge History of the Cold War*, vol. 2, *Crises and Détente*, edited by in Melvyn P. Leffler and O. A. Westad, 438–59. New York: Cambridge University Press, 2010.

Daniels, Roger. *Asian America: Chinese and Japanese in the United States since 1850*. Seattle: University of Washington Press, 1990.

Darnton, Robert. *The Forbidden Best-Sellers of Pre-Revolutionary France*. New York: W. W. Norton, 1995.

Demetz, Peter. *The Air Show at Brescia, 1909*. New York: Farrar, Straus, and Giroux, 2002.

Dennis-Tlwary, Tracy A. "Why Science Fiction Speaks the Language of Anxiety." *Psychology Today*, March 1, 2022. https://www.psychologytoday.com/us/blog/more-feeling/202203/why-science-fiction-speaks-the-language-anxiety.

de Syon, Guillaume. *Zeppelin! Germany and the Airship, 1900–1939*. Baltimore, MD: Johns Hopkins University Press, 2002.

DiPaolo, Marc, ed. *Working-Class Comic Book Heroes: Class Conflict and Populist Politics in Comics*. Jackson: University of Mississippi Press, 2018.

Disch, Thomas M. *The Dreams Our Stuff Is Made Of: How Science Fiction Conquered the World*. New York: Touchstone, 1998.

Dune Novels. Accessed October 12, 2023. https://dunenovels.com/.

Eisner, Will. *A Pictorial Arsenal of America's Combat Weapons*. New York: Sterling, 1960.

Ekstein, Modris. *Rites of Spring: The Great War and the Birth of the Modern Age*. New York: Anchor Books, 1989.

Encyclopedia of Science Fiction. "Herbert, Frank." September 12, 2022. https://sf-encyclopedia.com/entry/herbert_frank.

———. "Planetary Romance." December 4, 2013. https://sf-encyclopedia.com/entry/planetary_romance.

Encyclopedia of World Biography Online. "Hugo Gernsback." 2013. https://www.gale.com/ebooks/9781573029582/encyclopedia-of-world-biography-supplement

Engel, Joel. *Rod Serling: The Dreams and Nightmares of Life in the* Twilight Zone*: A Biography*. Chicago: Contemporary Books, 1989.

Erickson, Kai T. *Wayward Puritans: A Study in the Sociology of Deviance*. New York: Wiley, 1966.

Esposito, David. "'Abandon New York—Fall Back to Kansas City!' The Invasion Myth in American Culture." *Utopian Studies* 2, nos. 1–2 (1991): 114.

Evans, Arthur B. Introduction to *Invasion of the Sea* by Jules Verne. Middletown, CT: Wesleyan University Press, 2001.

Evans, Rebecca. "New Wave Science Fiction and the Dawn of the Environmental Movement." In *The Cambridge History of Science Fiction*, edited by Gerry Caravan and Eric Carl Link, 436–37. New York: Cambridge University Press, 2019.

Feingold, Henry. *Zion in America: The Jewish Experience from Colonial Times to the Present*. Mineola, NY: Dover, 2002.

Flanzbaum, Hilene, ed. *The Americanization of the Holocaust*. Baltimore, MD: Johns Hopkins University Press, 1999.

Ford, Carol. *Natural Interests: The Contest over Environment in Modern France*. Cambridge, MA: Harvard University Press, 2016.

———. "Reforestation, Landscape Conservation, and the Anxieties of Empire in French Colonial Algeria." *American Historical Review* 113, no. 2 (April 2008): 341–62.

Frayling, Christopher. *Mad, Bad and Dangerous? The Scientist and the Cinema*. London: Reaktion Books, 2005.

———. *Things to Come*. London: British Film Institute, 1995.

Fritz, Peter. *A Nation of Flyers: German Aviation and the Popular Imagination*. Cambridge, MA: Harvard University Press, 1992.

Fussell, Paul. *The Great War and Modern Memory*. New York: Oxford University Press, 1975.

Gibbons, Floyd. *The Red Napoleon*. New York: J. Cape and H. Smith, 1929.

Gleick, James. "The Making of Future Man." *New York Review of Books*, January 1, 2017.

Gollin, Alfred. "England Is No Longer an Island: The Phantom Airship Scare of 1909." *Albion* 13, no. 1 (Spring 1981): 43–57.

———. *The Impact of Air Power on the British People and Their Government, 1909–14*. Stanford, CA: Stanford University Press, 1989.

Gooch, John. "Attitudes to War in Late Victorian and Edwardian England." In *War and Society: A Yearbook of Military History*, edited by Brian Bond and Ian Roy, 88–102. New York: Holmes and Meier, 1975.

Greiner, Bernd. "'The Study of the Distant Past Is Futile': American Reflections on New Military Frontiers." In *The Shadows of Total War: Europe, East Asia, and the United States, 1919–1939*, edited by Roger Chickering and Stig Förster, 239–51. New York: German Historical Institute and Cambridge University Press, 2003.

Gunn, James. "Teaching Science Fiction." *Science Fiction Studies* 23, no. 70 (November 1996). https://www.depauw.edu/sfs/backissues/70/gunn70art.htm.

Hagens, Nate. "Kim Stanley Robinson: 'Climate, Fiction, and the Future': The Great Simplification #66." Video, 1:23:30. April 12, 2023. https://www.youtube.com/watch?v=Xc53KPv7flk&t=1280s.

Harpold, Terry. "European Science Fiction in the Nineteenth Century." In *The Cambridge History of Science Fiction*, edited by Gerry Canavan and Eric Carl Link, 50–68. New York: Cambridge University Press, 2019.

Hendershot, Cyndy. "Darwin and the Atom: Evolution/Devolution Fantasies in 'The Beast from 20,000 Fathoms,' 'Them!,' and "The Incredible Shrinking Man.'" *Science Fiction Studies* 25, no. 2 (July 1998): 319–35.

Henriksen, Margot A. *Dr. Strangelove's America: Society and Culture in the Atomic Age* Berkeley: University of California Press, 1997.

Higgins, David M. "New Wave Science Fiction and the Vietnam War." In *The Cambridge History of Science Fiction*, edited by Gerry Canavan and Eric Carl Link, 420–24. New York: Cambridge University Press, 2019.

Hinnant, Amanda, and Berkley Hudson. "The Magazine Revolution, 1880–1920." In *The Oxford History of Popular Print Culture*, vol. 6, *US Popular Print Culture, 1860–1920*, edited by Gary Kelly, 113–31. New York: Oxford University Press, 2012.

Hoberman, J. *An Army of Phantoms: American Movies and the Making of the Cold War*. New York: New Press, 2011.

Horowitz, Sara R. "Marge Piercy." Shalvi/Hyman Encyclopedia of Jewish Women. June 23, 2021. https://jwa.org/encyclopedia/article/piercy-marge.

Hutchings, Peter. "'We're the Martians Now': British Invasion Fantasies of the 1950s and 1960s." In *British Science Fiction Cinema*, edited by I. Q. Hunter (New York: Routledge, 1999).

Karlsen, Carol. *The Devil in the Shape of a Women: Witchcraft in Colonial New England*. New York: Norton, 1998.

Kennett, Lee B. *The First Air War, 1914–1918*. New York: Free Press, 1989.

Ketterer, David. "John Wyndham: The Facts of Life Sextet." In *A Companion to Science Fiction*, edited by David See, 375–77. Malden, MA: Blackwell 2008.

Kirkus Reviews. "Review of *The Forever War* by Joe Haldeman." November 1, 1974.

Krantz, Charles. "Teaching *Night and Fog*: History and Historiography." *Film and History: An Interdisciplinary Journal of Film and Television Studies* 15, no. 1 (February 1985): 1–11.

Krome, Frederic, ed. *Fighting the Future War: An Anthology of Science Fiction War Stories, 1914–1945*. New York: Routledge, 2012.

———. "'Will the Germans Bombard New York?' Hugo Gernsback and the Future War Story." *Journal of Military History* 86, no. 1 (January 2022): 54–76.

Krome, Frederic, Phoebe Reeves, and Greg Loving. "The Concept of the Human in John Wyndham's *The Chrysalids*: Puritanical Imagery, Female Agency, and Theistic Evolution." *Interdisciplinary Humanities* 32, no. 2 (Summer 2015): 52–64.

Kunzru, Hari. "Dune 50 Years On: How a Science Fiction Novel Changed the World." *Guardian*, July 3, 2015. https://www.theguardian.com/books/2015/jul/03/dune-50-years-on-science-fiction-novel-world.

Langer, Lawrence. "The Americanization of the Holocaust on Stage and Screen." In *Admitting the Holocaust: Collected Essays*. New York: Oxford University Press, 1995.

Lear, Linda. *Rachel Carson: Witness for Nature*. New York: Henry Holt, 1997.

Lincoln, H. Bruce. *War Stars: The Superweapon and the American Imagination*. New York: Oxford University Press, 1988.

Linn, Brian McAllister. *Elvis's Army: Cold War GIs and the Atomic Battlefield*. Cambridge, MA: Harvard University Press, 2016.

Liptak, Andrew. "Interview with Joe Haldeman." *Andrew Liptak* (blog), November 13, 2014. https://www.andrewliptak.com/blog/2014/11/13/interview-with-joe-haldeman.

Lottman, Herbert R. *Jules Verne: An Exploratory Biography*. New York: St. Martin's Press, 1996.

Luckhurst, Roger. *Science Fiction*. Cambridge, UK: Polity, 2005.

MacLeod, Ken. *The Star Fraction*. New York: Tor, 2001.

Masri, Heather. *Science Fiction: Stories and Contexts*. New York: Bedford/St. Martin's, 2008.

McConnell, Frank. *The Science Fiction of H. G. Wells*. New York: Oxford University Press, 1981.

McGregor, Donald, with Roy Thomas, Gerry Conway, Marv Wolfman, and Bill Mantlo. *Killraven: Warrior of the Worlds*. Vol. 1, *1973–1983*. New York: Marvel Worldwide, 2021.

McMeekin, Sean. *The Berlin-Baghdad Express: The Ottoman Empire and Germany's Bid for World Power*. Cambridge, MA: Harvard University Press, 2012.

Memmott, Mark. "75 Years Ago, 'War of the Worlds' Started a Panic. Or Did It?" NPR. October 30, 2013. https://www.npr.org/sections/thetwo-way/2013/10/30/241797346/75-years-ago-war-of-the-worlds-started-a-panic-or-did-it.

Michaelson, Jay. "Golem: Making Men of Clay: Can Imitating God Extend to the Creative Realm?" My Jewish Learning. Accessed October 12, 2023. https://www.myjewishlearning.com/article/golem/.

Mollmann, Steven. "*The War of the Worlds* in the *Boston Post* and the Rise of American Imperialism: 'Let Mars Fire.'" *English Literature in Transition* 53, no. 4 (2010): 387–412.

National Museum of American History. "Black Panther, Vol. 1 No. 4." Smithsonian. Accessed October 12, 2023. https://www.si.edu/object/black-panther-vol-1-no-4%3Anmah_1894264.

Novick, Peter. *The Holocaust in American Life*. Boston: Houghton Mifflin, 1999.

Nuttall, Christopher. "The Quiet Diversity of Robert Anson Heinlein." Mad Genius Club. January 3, 2018. https://madgeniusclub.com/2018/01/03/the-quiet-diversity-of-robert-anson-heinlein-by-christopher-nuttall/.

O'Falt, Chris. "Paul Verhoeven Slams 'Starship Troopers' Remake, Says It'll Be a Fascist Update Perfect for a Trump Presidency." IndieWire. November 16, 2016. https://www.indiewire.com/2016/11/paul-verhoeven-slams-starship-troopers-remake-fascist-update-perfect-trump-presidency-1201747155/.

Ort, Thomas. *Art and Life in Modernist Prague: Karol Čapek and His Generation, 1911–1938*. New York: Palgrave Macmillan, 2013.

Overy, Richard. *The Morbid Age: Britain between the Wars*. London: Allen Lane, 2009.

Palmer, Scott W. *Dictatorship of the Air: Aviation Culture and the Fate of Modern Russia*. New York: Cambridge University Press, 2006.

Patterson, William H., Jr. *Robert A. Heinlein: In Dialogue with His Century*. Volume 2 *1948–1988: The Man Who Learned Better*. New York: Tor Books, 2014.

Pick, Daniel. *War Machine: The Rationalisation of Slaughter in the Modern Age*. New Haven, CT: Yale University Press, 1993.
Prado, John. *Vietnam: The History of an Unwinnable War, 1945–1975*. Lawrence: University Press of Kansas 2009.
Ransom, Amy J. "The First Last Man: Cousin de Grainville's *Le Dernier homme*." *Science Fiction Studies* 41, no. 2 (July 2014): 314–40.
Remarque, Erich Maria. *All Quiet on the Western Front*. Translated by A. W. Wheen. London: G. P. Putnam's Sons, 1929.
Richardson, Jacques. "Future War and Superweapons: The Perceptive Fantasies of Albert Robida." *Foresight's* 9, no. 6 (2007): 61–73.
Roberts, Adam. "First Men and Original Sins." *Image*, no. 101 (Summer 2019). https://imagejournal.org/article/first-men-and-original-sins/.
———. *H. G. Wells: A Literary Life*. New York: Palgrave Macmillan, 2019.
———. *The History of Science Fiction*. New York: Palgrave Macmillan, 2005.
Robinson, Frank M., and Lawrence Davidson. *Pulp Culture: The Art of the Fiction Magazine*. Portland, OR: Collectors Press, 2001.
Robinson, Kim Stanley. "Empty Half the Earth of Its Humans. It's the Only Way to Save the Planet." *Guardian*, March 20, 2018. https://www.theguardian.com/cities/2018/mar/20/save-the-planet-half-earth-kim-stanley-robinson.
Rose, Alexander. *Empires of the Sky: Zeppelins, Airplanes, and Two Men's Epic Duel to Rule the World*. New York: Random House, 2020.
Rosenfeld, Gavriel D. "Why Do We Ask 'What If?' Reflections on the Function of Alternate History." *History and Theory*, theme issue 41 (December 2002): 90–103.
———. *The World Hitler Never Made: Alternate History and the Memory of Nazism*. New York: Cambridge University Press, 2005.
Rottensteiner, Franz, ed. *The Black Mirror and Other Stories: An Anthology of Science Fiction from Germany and Austria*. Translated by Mike Mitchell. Middletown, CT: Wesleyan University Press, 2008.
Sawyer, Andy, and Peter Wright, eds. *Teaching Science Fiction*. New York: Palgrave Macmillan, 2011.
Scalzi, John. *Whatever: Furiously Reasonable* (blog). Accessed October 12, 2023. https://whatever.scalzi.com/.
Schachner, Nat. *The Price of Liberty: A History of the American Jewish Committee*. New York: American Jewish Committee, 1948.
———. "Pulp Authors Have a Job to Do." *Writer* (August 1945).
Schaub, Michael. "'Sad Puppies' Campaign Fails to Undermine Sci-Fi Diversity at the Hugo Awards." *Los Angeles Times*, August 24, 2015. https://www.latimes.com/books/jacketcopy/la-et-jc-no-love-for-sad-puppies-hugo-awards-20150824-story.html.
Seed, David. *American Science Fiction and the Cold War: Literature and Film*. Chicago: Fitzroy and Dearborn, 1999.
———. *Science Fiction: A Very Short Introduction*. New York: Oxford University Press, 2011.

———. "The Strategic Defense Initiative: A Utopian Fantasy." In *Future Wars: The Anticipations and the Fears*, edited by David Seed, 184–85. Liverpool, UK: Liverpool University Press, 2012.

Sethness, Javier. "Toward and Ecologically Based Post-Capitalism: Interview with Novelist Kim Stanley Robinson." Truthout. March 17, 2018. https://truthout.org/articles/toward-an-ecologically-based-post-capitalism-interview-with-novelist-kim-stanley-robinson/.

Shandler, Jeffrey. "Aliens in the Wasteland: American Encounters with the Holocaust on 1960s Science Fiction Television." In *The Americanization of the Holocaust*, edited by Hilene Flanzbaum, 33–44. Baltimore, MD: Johns Hopkins University Press, 1999.

———. *While America Watches: Televising the Holocaust*. New York: Oxford University Press, 2000.

Shaw, Tony, and Denise J. Youngblood. *Cinematic Cold War: The American and Soviet Struggle for Hearts and Minds*. Lawrence: University Press of Kansas, 2010.

Shephard, W. Andrew. "Afrofuturism in the Nineteenth and Twentieth Centuries." In *The Cambridge History of Science Fiction*, edited by Gerry Canavan and Eric Carl Link, 101–19. New York: Cambridge University Press, 2019.

Showalter, Dennis E. "Heinlein's *Starship Troopers*: An Exercise in Rehabilitation." *Extrapolation* 16, no.2 (1974): 113–24.

Smith, Andrew Alan. "Jack Kirby: The Not-So-Secret Identity of the Thing." In *Working-Class Comic Book Heroes: Class Conflict and Populist Politics in Comics*, edited by Marc DiPaolo, 195–201. University of Mississippi Press, 2018.

Smith, David C., ed. *The Correspondence of H. G. Wells*. Vol. 3, *1919–1934*. London: Pickering and Chatto, 1998.

———. *H. G. Wells: Desperately Mortal*. New Haven, CT: Yale University Press, 1986.

Smith, Paul, ed. *The Historian and Film*. New York: Cambridge University Press, 1976.

Sontag, Susan. "The Imagination of Disaster." *Commentary* (October 1965): 42–48.

Sterling, Bruce. Preface to *Burning Chrome*, by William Gibson. New York: HarperCollins, 1986.

Stites, Richard. *Revolutionary Dreams: Utopian Vision and Experimental Life in the Russian Revolution*. New York: Oxford University Press, 1989.

Telotte, J. P. "In the Cinematic Zone of the *Twilight Zone*." *Science Fiction Film and Television* 3, no. 1 (2010): 10–13.

Times [London]. "Mr. Baldwin on Aerial Warfare: A Fear for the Future." November 11, 1932, 7.

Travers, T. H. E. "H. G. Wells and British Military Theory, 1895–1916." In *War and Society: A Yearbook of Military History*, edited by Brian Bond and Ian Roy, 67–87. New York: Holms and Meier, 1975.

Van Riper, A. Bowdoin. *Teaching History with Science Fiction Films*. Lanham, MD: Rowman and Littlefield, 2017.

Wagar, W. Warren. *H. G. Wells: Traversing Time*. Middletown, CT: Wesleyan University Press, 2004.

Whitfield, Stephen J. "Shoah." In *In Search of American Jewish Culture*. Hanover, NH: University Press of New England, 1999.

Wikipedia. "Cyberpunk." Updated October 7, 2023. https://en.wikipedia.org/wiki/Cyberpunk.

———. "Sad Puppies." Updated July 12, 2023. https://en.wikipedia.org/wiki/Sad_Puppies.

———. "*Southern Victory*." Updated July 18, 2023. https://en.wikipedia.org/wiki/Southern_Victory.

Winter, Denis. *The First of the Few: Fighter Pilots of the First World War*. Athens: University of Georgia Press, 1983.

Winter, Jay. *Remembering War: The Great War Between Memory and History in the Twentieth Century*. New Haven, CT: Yale University Press, 2006.

———. *Sites of Memory, Sites of Mourning: The Great War in European Cultural History*. New York: Cambridge University Press, 1995.

Wohl, Robert. *A Passion for Wings: Aviation and the Western Imagination, 1908–1918*. New Haven, CT: Yale University Press, 1994.

———. *The Spectacle of Flight: Aviation and the Western Imagination, 1920–1950*. New Haven, CT: Yale University Press, 2005.

Wolfe, Gary K. *The Known and the Unknown: The Iconography of Science Fiction*. Kent, OH: Kent State University Press, 1979.

About the Author

Frederic Krome earned his PhD in history from the University of Cincinnati in 1992. From 1992 to 1998, he taught at Northern Kentucky University, before becoming managing editor of the *American Jewish Archives Journal* at Hebrew Union College. In addition to his editorial role, he was an adjunct instructor of history and Judaic studies in the Arts and Sciences College of the University of Cincinnati. In 2007, he joined the faculty at the University of Cincinnati Clermont College, where he is now a professor of history.

Professor Krome regularly uses science fiction in his teaching and research. His edited volume *Fighting the Future War: An Anthology of Science Fiction War Stories, 1914–1945* (2011) provides an extensive introduction on science fiction as a valuable primary source. He has also published extensively on a variety of topics, ranging from Anglo-American film propaganda during World War II to the evolution of modern Jewish historical consciousness, in such journals as *Historian*, *Journal of Contemporary History*, *Modern Judaism*, and *Jewish History*. His most recent article, "Will the Germans Bombard New York? Hugo Gernsback and the Future War Tale," was published in the January 2022 issue of the *Journal of Military History*. He has also published more than two hundred book reviews and is a regular reviewer for *Choice Magazine*.

www.ingramcontent.com/pod-product-compliance
Lightning Source LLC
Chambersburg PA
CBHW032216230426
43672CB00011B/2573